The
Titanic

The Titanic

Dan Harmon

CHELSEA HOUSE PUBLISHERS
Philadelphia

Cover photos: Corbis/Bettmann-UPI; Archive Photo

CHELSEA HOUSE PUBLISHERS

Editor in Chief Stephen Reginald
Production Manager Pamela Loos
Art Director Sara Davis
Director of Photography Judy L. Hasday
Managing Editor James D. Gallagher
Senior Production Editor J. Christopher Higgins

Staff for THE *TITANIC*

Associate Art Director/Designer Takeshi Takahashi
Picture Researcher Patricia Burns
Cover Designer Takeshi Takahashi

First Printing

1 3 5 7 9 8 6 4 2

The Chelsea House World Wide Web address is
http://www.chelseahouse.com

Library of Congress Cataloging-in-Publication Data

Harmon, Daniel E.
The Titanic / by Daniel Harmon.
   p. cm. — (Great Disasters: Reforms and Ramifications)
Includes bibliographical references.
Summary: Describes the large luxury liner that sunk after
colliding with an iceberg in 1912, focusing on the lifeboat rescue of the surviving passengers and the inquiry after the
tragedy that brought about additional regulations in maintaining safety on passenger ships.

ISBN 0-7910-5265-6 (hc)

1. Titanic (Steamship) Juvenile literature. 2. Shipwrecks—
North Atlantic Ocean Juvenile literature. [1. Titanic
(Steamship) 2. Shipwrecks.] I. Title. II. Series.
G530.T6H36 2000
910'.91634—dc21   99-23647
                                         CIP

Contents

Introduction
Jill McCaffrey   7

1 An Avoidable Disaster   11

2 Speed, Comfort, Safety, and Ice   19

3 Farewell to England   33

4 "Iceberg! Dead Ahead!"   47

5 Rescue   67

6 Placing the Blame, or
       Making Excuses?   81

7 A Safer Ocean   97

Chronology of *Titanic*'s History   112
Chronology of *Titanic*'s Maiden Voyage   113
Further Reading   114
Index   116

GREAT DISASTERS
REFORMS and RAMIFICATIONS

THE *APOLLO ONE* AND
CHALLENGER DISASTERS

THE BLIZZARD OF 1888

THE BOMBING OF HIROSHIMA

THE *EXXON VALDEZ*

THE GREAT CHICAGO FIRE

THE *HINDENBURG*

THE HOLOCAUST

THE INFLUENZA PANDEMIC OF 1918

THE JOHNSTOWN FLOOD

PEARL HARBOR

THE SAN FRANCISCO EARTHQUAKE
OF 1906

THE STOCK MARKET CRASH OF 1929

TERRORISM

THREE MILE ISLAND

THE *TITANIC*

THE TRIANGLE SHIRTWAIST COMPANY
FIRE OF 1911

Jill McCaffrey

National Chairman,
Armed Forces Emergency Services
American Red Cross

Introduction

Disasters have always been a source of fascination and awe. Tales of a great flood that nearly wipes out all life are among humanity's oldest recorded stories, dating at least from the second millennium B.C., and they appear in cultures from the Middle East to the Arctic Circle to the southernmost tip of South America and the islands of Polynesia. Typically gods are at the center of these ancient disaster tales—which is perhaps not too surprising, given the fact that the tales originated during a time when human beings were at the mercy of natural forces they did not understand.

To a great extent, we still are at the mercy of nature, as anyone who reads the newspapers or watches nightly news broadcasts can attest. Hurricanes, earthquakes, tornados, wildfires, and floods continue to exact a heavy toll in suffering and death, despite our considerable knowledge of the workings of the physical world. If science has offered only limited protection from the consequences of natural disasters, it has in no way diminished our fascination with them. Perhaps that's because the scale and power of natural disasters force us as individuals to confront our relatively insignificant place in the physical world and remind us of the fragility and transience of our lives. Perhaps it's because we can imagine ourselves in the midst of dire circumstances and wonder how we would respond. Perhaps it's because disasters seem to bring out the best and worst instincts of humanity: altruism and selfishness, courage and cowardice, generosity and greed.

As one of the national chairmen of the American Red Cross, a humanitarian organization that provides relief for victims of disasters, I have had the privilege of seeing some of humanity's best instincts. I have witnessed communities pulling together in the face of trauma; I have seen thousands of people answer the call to help total strangers in their time of need.

Of course, helping victims after a tragedy is not the only way, or even the best way, to deal with disaster. In many cases planning and preparation can minimize damage and loss of life—or even avoid a disaster entirely. For, as history repeatedly shows, many disasters are caused not by nature but by human folly, shortsightedness, and unethical conduct. For example, when a land developer wanted to create a lake for his exclusive resort club in Pennsylvania's Allegheny Mountains in 1880, he ignored expert warnings and cut corners in reconstructing an earthen dam. On May 31, 1889, the dam gave way, unleashing 20 million tons of water on the towns below. The Johnstown Flood, the deadliest in American history, claimed more than 2,200 lives. Greed and negligence would figure prominently in the Triangle Shirtwaist Company fire in 1911. Deplorable conditions in the garment sweatshop, along with a failure to give any thought to the safety of workers, led to the tragic deaths of 146 persons. Technology outstripped wisdom only a year later, when the designers of the luxury liner *Titanic* smugly declared their state-of-the-art ship "unsinkable," seeing no need to provide lifeboat capacity for everyone onboard. On the night of April 14, 1912, more than 1,500 passengers and crew paid for this hubris with their lives after the ship collided with an iceberg and sank. But human catastrophes aren't always the unforeseen consequences of carelessness or folly. In the 1940s the leaders of Nazi Germany purposefully and systematically set out to exterminate all Jews, along with Gypsies, homosexuals, the mentally ill, and other so-called undesirables. More recently terrorists have targeted random members of society, blowing up airplanes and buildings in an effort to advance their political agendas.

The books in the GREAT DISASTERS: REFORMS AND RAMIFICATIONS series examine these and other famous disasters, natural and human made. They explain the causes of the disasters, describe in detail how events unfolded, and paint vivid portraits of the people caught up in dangerous circumstances. But these books are more than just accounts of what happened to whom and why. For they place the disasters in historical perspective, showing how people's attitudes and actions changed and detailing the steps society took in the wake of each calamity. And in the end, the most important lesson we can learn from any disaster—as well as the most fitting tribute to those who suffered and died—is how to avoid a repeat in the future.

An Avoidable Disaster

I t was the largest—and supposedly safest—ship ever built. Its owners pronounced it unsinkable. The ship boasted numerous features that seemed to back up their claim:

In her construction and maintenance were involved every science, profession, and trade known to civilization. On her bridge were officers, who, besides being the pick of the Royal Navy, had passed rigid examinations in all studies that pertained to the winds, tides, currents, and geography of the sea; they were not only seamen, but scientists. The same professional standard applied to the personnel of the engine-room, and the steward's department was equal to that of a first-class hotel.

From bow to stern, the vessel was divided into compartments separated by heavy walls, called bulkheads, with watertight doors. In the event of a collision, the compartments could be quickly sealed off from each other to prevent incoming water from flooding the entire hull. Even if some of the compartments flooded, the ship would stay afloat: according to the ship's promoters, "no known accident of the sea" could possibly fill more than one or two compartments at once.

Safety features aside, this boat was a luxury liner. Every convenience and entertainment was provided for first-class passengers: brass bands, string orchestras, theater, fine dining, and games. Doctors and ministers attended the travelers' physical and spiritual needs. The spectacular view afforded by the great ship was a luxury unto itself. The open decks were a short walk from the travelers' cabins. Passengers could see miles of majestic ocean and sky on the horizon. On a cold, clear April evening, it seemed that they could see every star in the sky.

It was on just such a cold April night that this massive, "unsinkable" luxury liner, which sped across the Atlantic Ocean at a speed of 24 knots (more than 20 miles an hour), struck an iceberg and sank. There weren't nearly enough lifeboats for the passengers and crew, since no one had believed that lifeboats would ever be needed. More than a thousand voyagers went down with the great ship.

Is this the tragic story of *Titanic,* the fabled liner swallowed by the North Atlantic during the predawn hours of April 15, 1912? Despite its striking similarities to a disaster that would inspire numerous books, several movies, and a Broadway musical, this tale was actually written nearly 14 years before *Titanic*'s doomed voyage. A veteran seafarer named Morgan Robertson, who was all too familiar with the unsafe conditions of passenger vessels at the turn of the century, wrote a novel about a great sea disaster in 1899.

Not too many years after the publication of Morgan Robertson's popular novel, newspaper reporters were singing the praises of the real-life *Titanic* as they anticipated its maiden voyage from Southampton, England, to New York City in April of 1912. Various observers of *Titanic* expressed their awe of the great vessel, calling it "a golden coach for millionaires," "the marvel of the 20th century," "a vast floating city," and "a wonder ship." *Titanic*'s owner, the White Star Line, called it "a floating palace."

The RMS *Titanic* ("RMS" stands for "royal mail ship") was 882.5 feet long and 92.5 feet wide, and it weighed more than 45,000 tons. Construction on *Titanic* began in 1909 in Belfast, Ireland, and it took 3,000 workers nearly three years to build the gigantic vessel. The ship was the height of an 11-story building—175 feet from the keel (bottom) to the tops of its funnels—and about four city blocks long. Some three million rivets held together the heavy steel plates of its hull. Constructed at a cost of $10 million, the ship was the largest man-made moving object ever built up to that time.

Titanic's rudder alone weighed 100 tons. (*Nina*, one of Columbus's three ships in 1492, weighed a total of only 60 tons from end to end; the Pilgrims' *Mayflower* had a total tonnage of about 180.) Each link in *Titanic*'s anchor chain weighed as much as a strong, healthy

Called a "floating palace," *Titanic* boasted elaborate rooms, such as the bedroom shown above, and a grand staircase (at right). The luxurious accommodations impressed all who sailed on the ship's maiden voyage.

man. It took 20 draft horses to pull the anchor through Belfast's streets to the shipyard. Each of the vessel's engines was the size of a three-story house.

As with Robertson's imaginary liner, the steel-hulled *Titanic* was divided into watertight compartments. One command from the ship's bridge could seal the compartments off from each other, securing the vessel from widespread flooding in the event of an accident. Like Robertson's fictional ship, *Titanic* could remain afloat and navigable even if two of its compartments flooded at the same time. For an extra measure of safety, *Titanic* had a double bottom, with concrete

poured between the two layers of steel.

The ship's builders concentrated on safeguarding *Titanic* against typical shipping accidents: running aground or striking another ship. The reinforced bottom and watertight bulkheads were more than adequate to absorb these types of collisions. If *Titanic*'s side was pierced, simply closing the watertight doors would contain the flooding to the damaged compartment. With these safety features, *Titanic*'s builders reasoned that in a collision with a smaller ship—all other ships were smaller than *Titanic* at the time—the liner would suffer only minor damage.

The great liner's list of luxury features was even more exhaustive than the number of features designed for safety. Before the advent of luxury liners in the early 20th century, ocean travel had often been a miserable ordeal. Aboard *Titanic*, it was designed to be a vacation at sea. For first-class passengers, a swimming pool, gym, steam bath, and exquisite dining with the finest china and stemware awaited. In the event of a passenger's injury or illness, the ship offered a hospital complete with surgical facilities. In addition to deck games, a full squash court was available to gentlemen who wanted to stay trim during their Atlantic holiday.

A grand central staircase was reminiscent of those found in the finest hotels in Europe. First-class passengers could relax in a lounge patterned after the interior of the French royal palace at Versailles. The first-class bedrooms and baths resembled those found in an elegant present-day bed-and-breakfast inn.

The opulence didn't end with first class, however. Seasoned ocean travelers who booked second-class berths on *Titanic* reported that their accommodations were nicer than those of first-class cabins in many rival liners. Like the men in first class, those in second class had their own barber shop. Second-class travelers also enjoyed a spacious, comfortable lounge/library and a smoking room. The ship provided even third-class passengers with a "general room," or lounge, with teak furniture. These passengers, too, had a smoking room. The food at every level was excellent.

After the ship was completed in the spring of 1912, the White Star Line advertised its maiden voyage from Southampton, England. Some of the most affluent families of the Western world—the Astors, Strauses,

Wideners, Guggenheims, and other names synonymous with success—booked passage on the maiden voyage.

Perhaps some of the passengers had read Morgan Robertson's novel. There is no record, however, that anyone ever made a connection between *Titanic* and the name of Robertson's fictitious luxury superliner. Robertson had turned to Greek mythology to find a name befitting the huge, splendid vessel of his novel— just as officials of the White Star Steamship Line would years later. Robertson called his tragic ship *Titan*.

The competition for passengers drove trans-atlantic shipping companies to build bigger, faster, and more luxurious ships. These features were emphasized in advertisements of the day, such as this White Star Line poster, which calls *Titanic* and its sister ship *Olympic* "the largest steamers in the world."

Speed, Comfort, Safety, and Ice

Although commercial passage to America had begun centuries earlier, until the mid-19th century the very idea of an Atlantic crossing was enough to make one seasick. Ocean travel was expensive, dangerous, and extremely unpleasant. The quarters were stifling; the food, repulsive. Storms rocked little vessels mercilessly as passengers held on for dear life. Many a ship foundered at sea, never to be heard from again. Even sailing through coastal waters from one seaport to another was a gamble. The main objective was not so much that a ship arrive on time, but just that it arrive safely. For a vessel to sail into port a day or even a week late was not uncommon. Nor was it unusual for months of waiting to drag by until a ship was finally reported missing.

The advent of steamships made the passage more predictable, because sea captains were no longer forced to depend on prevailing winds to push them to their destinations. By the 1860s, companies were offering cheap travel rates and promising reliable schedules.

The transatlantic shipping industry quickly grew very competitive. At first, shipping companies could do a brisk business simply by carrying people faster and at a lower cost than their competitors could. By the 1890s, however, it was clear that passengers expected something more: they wanted to travel in comfort and style.

In the early 20th century, two great British steamship companies led the race for transatlantic business: the Cunard Line and the White Star Line. Early in the century, two splendid, state-of-the-art Cunard ships, *Lusitania* and *Mauretania*, caught the public's eye. These "sister ships" were gigantic, luxurious, and fast. *Lusitania* was 790 feet long. *Mauretania* was the world's fastest ship until the 1920s.

German shipping companies were producing superliners as big and swift as those made by the British. Although shipping companies in France, Italy, Sweden, and other nations sought the business of both upper-class travelers and immigrants who booked cheap passage in steerage (third class), the competition was especially intense between the German and English passenger lines.

White Star officials knew they had to come up with something better than their German rivals and the ships of the Cunard Line. They formulated plans for three sister ships, floating wonderlands larger and more luxurious than *Lusitania* and *Mauretania*. They would call them *Olympic*, *Titanic*, and *Gigantic*. (The name of the third ship, which was launched after *Titanic* sank, was changed to *Britannic* before its first voyage. In light of the *Titanic* disaster, the company decided that being British was a much safer claim to fame than being big.)

Titanic and *Olympic* were built side by side in the Belfast shipyards. The slightly smaller *Olympic* was launched in the autumn of 1910, seven months before *Titanic*. The ships were so spectacular and the public so eager to see them that tickets were sold to their launching ceremonies. The thousands who attended *Titanic*'s launching—shortly after noon on May 31, 1911—were in for a brief show. It took approximately one minute for the monstrous ship's weight to carry it down a set of greased tracks and into the harbor as it strained against the chains that were attached to hold it back.

Although the main structure was completed, it took workers another 10 months to finish the interior. On April 2, 1912, *Titanic* was ready for a quick sea trial. As expected, it passed with flying colors. A week later, the ship was ready to set forth on its maiden voyage.

Once *Titanic* was at sea, the pressure to sustain the public's interest in the great ship may have intensified. For years, historians have been divided over whether *Titanic*'s captain, Edward J. Smith, had been urged by his employers to break a speed record on the maiden voyage—or at least to arrive at New York sooner than scheduled. The White Star Line knew the value of sensational publicity. If *Titanic* could surprise the world on its first voyage by reaching New York earlier than scheduled, banner headlines would be assured. But reputable liner captains almost never took such risks. Smith had earned his distinguished record of command

The hulls of *Titanic* and *Olympic* were constructed next to one another in the Harland and Wolff shipyard in Belfast, Ireland.

through steady caution over many years.

Besides, *Titanic* wasn't the fastest ship on the water. Other liners could beat its top speed of about 25 nautical miles per hour ("knots"). Its designers never expected *Titanic* to set an Atlantic crossing record. Instead, they had wanted to create the finest, most memorable ocean vacation people could take. They also wanted it to be dependable and punctual, maintaining its schedule in all kinds of weather, departing and arriving almost on the minute. Its average speed of 21 knots was more than adequate to please the most demanding customers. (By comparison, the Cunard liner *Carpathia* placidly cruised the Atlantic at about 14 knots.)

Even if *Titanic*'s captain wasn't racing to beat his schedule, he was mindful that he must remain on time. Ocean tides determined the hours during which large ships could safely enter harbors. Tides rise and fall twice daily. Therefore an hour's delay approaching port could mean half a day's additional wait for the next rising tide until the ship could dock and discharge passengers. And all North Atlantic superliner captains drove their ships briskly through the cold waters, even near the fringes of the Arctic ice packs. They were caught up in the competition for passengers, which was fiercer than ever in 1912.

To poor citizens of Europe and other continents, turn-of-the-century America was the land of dreams. More than 13 million new settlers arrived in the United States between 1900 and 1914. Most came from Europe, and most entered at the port of New York, creating a lot of business for shipping companies.

By 1912, though, the big passenger lines weren't looking to make their biggest profits from poor steerage passengers. Their new luxury ships were intended to attract the growing upper class, wealthy travelers who had made fortunes during the Industrial Revolution. It was the country's fabled Gilded Age. American industrial tycoons frequently took their families abroad to vacation on the French Riviera or to visit other countries. These first-class passengers were the shipping lines' target market. They were accustomed to the finest of everything. When traveling, they demanded the latest creature comforts and entertainments (not to mention speedy voyages).

However, to any traveler planning to cross the Atlantic in spring 1912, *Titanic* seemed by far the safest ship available. White Star Line officials proudly called it "unsinkable." The public realized *Titanic* was no ordinary ship, and accepted the company's boast as a hard fact rather than an advertising claim. There were several reasons for this. First, *Titanic* was the largest vessel ever built—in fact, it was the largest moving object in existence on land or sea. It was hard to imagine that anything so colossal could suffer significant damage at sea. In a collision with any other vessel, *Titanic* surely would have emerged barely scarred. Observers were certain the ship would be at sea long after they were dead.

Also, *Titanic* was designed to be unsinkable. For years, shipbuilders had used strong, waterproof bulkheads to divide ships into compartments. In *Titanic*, a series of massive steel bulkheads divided the hull into 16 watertight compartments. In an emergency, each one of these could be sealed off. They extended from the keel of the ship upward for several decks—but did not go as high as the main deck. In theory, any two of the main compartments could be flooded, and the ship would remain afloat. It was inconceivable to *Titanic*'s designers that a collision at sea might affect more than two compartments.

The ship's designers were confident that the towering, watertight bulkheads within *Titanic*'s hull would keep the ship from sinking. If the hull sustained a puncture, flooding would be contained by an individual compartment's steel walls. The amount of water pouring into one or two ruptured compartments would not be enough to drag down the vessel.

As it turned out, the bulkheads were no guarantee of safety. Unfortunately, the ship's designers had not anticipated a collision with an iceberg that would slice open the hull across five compartments simultaneously. Also, the bulkheads did not extend all the way up to the main deck. After the collision, the flooding of the forward compartments began dragging down the bow of the ship as sea water rose to the top of each bulkhead, then began spilling into each adjacent compartment. With multiple forward compartments pierced at once, the sea water rushed in faster than it could be pumped out, and it was only a matter of time before the relentless ocean pulled the ship's flooded bow below the surface.

But with all the advertised safety measures, word that E. J. Smith would be captain of *Titanic* on the maiden voyage may have inspired the most confidence in the ship. Captain Smith was the most experienced captain of the White Star Line, and his reputation for safety and caution was well known. He had never commanded a ship that had been sunk or badly damaged in an accident.

However, Captain Smith may have been too certain that the technology of the day had made *Titanic* indeed "unsinkable." When he had commanded *Adriatic* six years earlier, Smith had commented, "I cannot imagine any condition that would cause a [superliner] to founder. . . . Modern shipbuilding has gone beyond that."

Trusting in the strength of *Titanic*'s construction, perhaps he wasn't as concerned as he should have been about the peculiar dangers of northern shipping lanes. Perhaps he saw no need to reduce speed in the face of iceberg warnings.

It is important to remember that even though E. J. Smith was one of the most experienced captains on the sea, new liners like *Titanic* were larger than any ships ever built prior to that time. This presented new navigational difficulties. Several months before *Titanic*'s maiden voyage, her sister liner *Olympic*—under Smith's command—had been hit by the British Navy ship *Hawke* off the Isle of Wight. The two ships were moving parallel to each other when *Hawke* suddenly nosed into the side of *Olympic*. The reason, a board of inquiry determined, was the surprisingly strong suction created by *Olympic*. The large liner, which was under the command of a harbor pilot at the time, should have slowed down as the two ships drew near, officials ruled. Although no one was badly hurt, the damage to *Hawke* was significant. If nothing else, the accident should have demonstrated to the White Star Line's revered captain that the navigation and piloting of such large ships could present unusual challenges.

Perhaps too, overconfidence in the safety features built into the superliners lulled shipbuilders and inspectors into ignoring possible problems. Despite the development of watertight compartments and stronger hulls, some safety concerns that might have prevented *Titanic*'s sinking, or at least reduced the loss of life, were overlooked. Most important was the shortage of lifeboats and rafts. *Titanic* carried 16 lifeboats—eight boats along each side of the boat deck. It

also had eight "Englehardts," collapsible boats that could be lowered after the regular lifeboats in the event of a dire emergency.

Even if all the boats were launched successfully and each one filled with its maximum number of passengers, fewer than 1,200 people could be saved if the ship sank. *Titanic* could carry three times that many travelers. Why, then, so few lifeboats? It was assumed they would never be needed. The lifeboats were visible on deck primarily to inspire confidence among passengers. The fact that there weren't enough for everyone was seldom, if ever, questioned. Legally, *Titanic* met shipping regulations in terms of number of lifeboats. In fact, it exceeded requirements. The number of lifeboats a ship should carry was based on the vessel's tonnage,

(continued on p. 30)

This puncture in the side of *Olympic* was caused when the liner was hit by the British warship *Hawke* in 1911. *Olympic* was so large that as it passed *Hawke*, powerful suction pulled the smaller ship into the liner. This accident should have pointed out the tremendous difficulty of steering the behemoth liners.

TITANIC'S CAPTAIN

Captain Edward J. Smith, commander of Titanic.

In addition to her formidable size and many safety features, *Titanic* boasted a seemingly infallible sailor at the helm. Captain E. J. Smith had been a seaman since he was 14, and a ship's captain for 25 years. He was admiral of the White Star fleet and the highest-paid passenger line skipper on the ocean. Captains of rival Cunard liners received half his salary.

Smith had become accustomed to commanding each new White Star steamer on its maiden crossing. Because he commanded the White Star Line's finest vessels, he was called "the millionaire's captain." The 59-year-old planned to retire after *Titanic* returned to England from New York. The maiden voyage of this great ship would be the final accomplishment in his long and distinguished career.

Softspoken, cheerful, and kind, the fatherly Smith impressed practically all who met him. Junior officers felt honored to serve under his command. Many regular transatlantic passengers knew Captain Smith—or knew of his reputation—and arranged to travel aboard his ships whenever possible. Wealthy Americans and Europeans who regularly crossed the Atlantic for business or pleasure knew Smith personally and respected him deeply. A young *Titanic* survivor would remember him as "very large . . . very upright . . . very nice."

Remarkably, in all his years at sea, Smith had never sailed or steamed aboard a vessel that was lost or heavily damaged. With a safety record like his, the good Smith was indeed a "captain's captain." But Smith's impeccable safety record—as well as *Titanic*'s size and special features—may have inspired a false sense of confidence that ultimately proved fatal. Because the ship was so long, *Titanic* needed more seaway and time to turn than smaller ships. After the iceberg was sighted in the darkness, there were precious few moments to change course. Despite frantic efforts to turn, the big ship was only beginning to veer away when it struck the ice.

Furthermore, Captain Smith's unblemished record and inspiring personality may have led the White Star Line to expect too much. He, of all its commanders, seemed best able to exceed public expectations on the ship's maiden voyage. Some historians have suggested that Smith was under strong pressure from White Star Line officials to go faster than he wanted and to take slight risks in his navigation. *Titanic*'s unexpected arrival in New York Harbor on Tuesday night, instead of on Wednesday morning as scheduled, would have generated valuable publicity for the shipping company.

The question of whether Smith was being urged to exceed safe speeds in an ice zone is one of many controversies debated by *Titanic* historians. Some doubt that any captain on his final voyage before retiring would risk a long, excellent record. Smith had little to gain and everything to lose by endangering the great ship and the lives entrusted to his command. Others are not so sure. They point out that although Smith was among the most experienced captains in service, not even he was entirely familiar with the ways of the new monster vessels.

Icebergs were a constant danger to ships in the North Atlantic. Only about one-tenth of the iceberg can be seen above the waterline; the remaining nine-tenths is submerged, posing a great hazard to any vessel that comes nearby. This may in fact be the iceberg that sank *Titanic*; it was the largest berg in the area when rescue ships arrived, and observers noted a smear of red paint—possibly from *Titanic*'s hull scraping against the ice—near the berg's waterline.

(continued from p. 27)

not on the number of passengers it could carry.

The rich passengers who traveled the Atlantic on the large ships of the White Star Line often took safety for granted and did not worry about the problems of navigation. However, the tricks to navigating the fastest course through the North Atlantic were of particular concern to ship captains. Posing an especially difficult problem, particularly in the spring, were icebergs that broke off from the polar ice cap and drifted south into the shipping lanes.

What are icebergs, exactly? The North Pole is not a land mass covered by ice; it is actually an ocean covered by ice. The ice cap over the Arctic Ocean has existed for ages. It never melts completely, but it changes with the seasons. Every spring, massive chunks of ice break away from the edges of the ice cap. Some of these chunks break into large, tall formations—icebergs. These large chunks are carried away from the frigid ice cap by ocean currents.

Even today sailors must be mindful of icebergs, especially during spring. Collisions with them are rare nowadays, thanks to modern navigational devices that can detect them from miles away. But the menace of bergs, which is compounded by their unknown dimensions beneath the water's surface, is still not to be taken lightly.

The danger to passing ships was great. In 1913, the year after *Titanic*'s maiden voyage, William Laird McKinlay was aboard an Arctic exploration vessel, *Karluk*. He reported his observations as *Karluk*, moving through an eerie fog, entered the area where *Titanic* had sunk:

> The conditions were identical [to those encountered by *Titanic*]—all around us icebergs of every shape and size. We could only occasionally see them, but we knew how close they were from the echo of the ship's siren reverberating from the masses of ice. For days we steamed "Dead Slow Ahead," and once a sudden stopping and immediate reversal of the engines sent a staggering shudder through the ship, and those of us on deck could faintly glimpse the huge iceberg as it drifted majestically past.

Karluk was eventually trapped and crushed to pieces by the moving ice. Even though McKinlay and others aboard *Karluk* could see the deadly icebergs surrounding them, they could not do anything to save their ship. On the night *Titanic* sank, on the other hand, lookouts thought they were steaming across a clear sea. They spotted only a single iceberg. But it was enough to bring about the same end that would later befall *Karluk*.

Farewell to England

On April 10, 1912, *Titanic* steamed out of Southampton, England, to begin her maiden voyage.

Thousands of passengers, relatives, and well-wishers swarmed the quay at Southampton, England. Stewards lugged tons of baggage up the gangways. Hugs, handshakes, smiles, and tears were exchanged as far as the eye could see. Most passengers traveling in first class were embarking on a luxurious holiday. For them, *Titanic*'s departure was a delightful occasion. But many of those in steerage were leaving Europe forever in the hope of making a better life in America— knowing they might never return to their homelands or see their families. For them, the departure was heartbreaking.

It was noon on Wednesday, April 10, 1912. The great liner was set to cast off on her maiden transatlantic voyage. Travelers eagerly anticipated spending a glorious week at sea in the floating palace. They were scheduled to arrive in New York Harbor the following Wednesday morning.

First-class passengers paid more than $4,000 in 1912 dollars (the equivalent of $50,000 today) to stay in one of *Titanic*'s promenade suites. It was the most expensive first-class passage a rich traveler could buy. Of course, these successful men and women could afford it. The first-class list included men like Benjamin Guggenheim, whose family had amassed a $100 million fortune through mining, processing precious metals, and banking; Philadelphia streetcar magnate George D. Widener, who with his father had helped to establish United States Steel Corporation and the American Tobacco Company; and Isidor Straus, who had become a multimillionaire as owner of Macy's department store and was a former U. S. congressman and a national political advisor. George Widener was traveling with his wife and their 27-year-old son, Harry; Straus was accompanied by his wife, Ida.

By comparison, the cost of a ticket for third-class (steerage) passengers was only a few dollars, but for poor immigrants, this was a formidable cost. Some steerage passengers had sold everything they owned to buy a ticket, hoping to make a fresh start in America. Aboard *Titanic* they found that even on the humble third-class decks, the living quarters were nicer than those they were accustomed to at home.

The crew members were no better paid or treated than those men and women serving on other ocean liners. Nevertheless, they were proud of their positions aboard the world's largest, ritziest steamer. Charles Burgess, a baker on *Titanic* who served on many other luxury liners both before and after *Titanic*'s maiden voyage, called it "a beautiful, wonderful ship," more elegant in detail than its sister ship *Olympic* or competitors from the Cunard Line. "Take the dining saloon" said Burgess. "The *Olympic* didn't even have a carpet, but the *Titanic*—ah, you sank in it up to your knees. Then there's the furniture, so heavy you could hardly lift it."

Like the passengers, crew members eagerly anticipated this voyage. They knew they would one day be telling their wide-eyed grandchildren about their adventures aboard the greatest ship ever built. All the world had talked excitedly about *Titanic* for more than a year before it left England. Photographs of the ship and newsreels showing its construction left viewers amazed. Its launching and preparation for service was one of the top stories of the time.

The ship's band played gaily as *Titanic* moved away from dockside. Other ships in the harbor, dwarfed by the monstrous hull, sounded their whistles in salute.

For one of these ships, however, the salute set the scene for a nerve-racking near-disaster. *New York*, a much smaller transatlantic liner, was moored in the River Test when the outbound *Titanic* passed close by under the harbor pilot's command. Because the enormous ship displaced thousands of tons of water, *Titanic* created tremendous suction simply by moving. Before anyone realized what was happening, the powerful suction began to draw *New York* toward *Titanic*. The unseen force was so sudden and powerful that *New York*'s mooring cables snapped. The vessel's stern swung into the seaway toward *Titanic*'s port (left) side. A collision seemed certain.

Thinking quickly, *Titanic*'s pilot ordered the propeller on the port side of the vessel reversed. Water churned forward from the blades. Meanwhile, collision mats were hastily placed on the ship's endangered side. For the next minute, anxious onlookers stared silently. At last, the propeller's reversal, aided by tugboats that responded immediately to move *New York,* took effect. The drifting ship moved away, and *Titanic* resumed its course.

Contact had been avoided, but the incident was

As the *Olympic-Hawke* collision had illustrated, the great liners were so large that their passing created an incredibly powerful suction. As *Titanic* steamed through the River Test, under the control of a harbor pilot, this suction caused the liner *New York* to break free from its moorings and swing toward *Titanic*. Fortunately, a collision was avoided, and while tugboats moved *New York* away (pictured here), *Titanic* was able to depart.

frightening nonetheless. A *Titanic* passenger watching from an upper deck turned grimly to his daughter and said, "It's a bad omen." Four days later, the fear of powerful suction from the massive ship would compel terrified occupants of *Titanic*'s lifeboats to steer well clear of the sinking ship. Dozens of freezing swimmers would therefore lose their lives.

Titanic proceeded across the English Channel to the French port of Cherbourg, where it took on about 100 more passengers early in the evening. One of them was 47-year-old Colonel John Jacob Astor, who was returning to America with his pregnant 19-year-old bride Madeline. The Astor fortune was estimated at $150 million; in today's economy, John Jacob Astor would have been a billionaire. His grandfather had built the family fortune by developing a monopoly on fur trading in the early 19th century; Astor, a veteran of the Spanish-American War, contributed by building the Astoria, Knickerbocker, and St. Regis hotels in New York City.

Also boarding at Cherbourg was a fashionable couple, Sir Cosmo and Lady Duff-Gordon. Sir Cosmo was a member of Scottish nobility; Lady Duff-Gordon founded and operated a world-famous dressmaking enterprise with branches in New York, London, and Paris that sold fashionable clothing to the world's elite.

After leaving Cherbourg, *Titanic* steamed to Queenstown, a port on the southern coast of Ireland. When it arrived the next day, *Titanic* was too large to tie up at the Queenstown dock; small boats brought out an additional 113 passengers bound for New York. *Titanic* steamed away from Queenstown on April 11 with some 2,210 people aboard, about 900 of them crew members. To White Star officials, this was a disappointment: they had hoped for a full complement of 3,000 passengers for *Titanic*'s maiden voyage.

The first day out *Titanic* logged a pleasing 484 miles. Captain Smith was satisfied that all was running smoothly. Aided by continuing fair weather, he increased the ship's speed. The total run on the second day, 519 miles, was posted on the ship's bulletin board. Some of the passengers were sufficiently impressed to begin making bets on the ship's daily progress and on

Titanic's first-class passenger list included many of the richest and most powerful people of the period.
Even among such a distinguished list, multi-millionaire John Jacob Astor stood out. Astor is shown here with his wife, Madeline.

the day and time of its arrival in New York.

Captain Smith may have felt pressure for a fast crossing from passengers. He also may have been urged by the managing director of the White Star Line, J. Bruce Ismay, to make a headline-grabbing maiden voyage. Ismay was one of *Titanic*'s most avid promoters. But even if he never ordered the captain to increase speed, his very presence would have conveyed silent

J. Bruce Ismay, managing director of the White Star Line, was aboard *Titanic* during the ill-fated maiden voyage. Ismay may have pressured Captain E. J. Smith to set a new speed record for an Atlantic crossing, which would increase *Titanic*'s fame and bring publicity to the shipping company.

pressure to make the best time possible.

For the passengers, the first days aboard *Titanic* passed pleasantly. In first class, the Wideners, Strauses, and Astors were joined by many notable passengers, including Major Archibald Butt, a writer and diplomat who was serving as a military aide to President William Howard Taft. Butt was returning to Washington from Italy, where he had visited the Pope on the president's behalf. Famous painter, author, and translator Francis David Millet was a colorful character. Charles M. Hays was a railroad baron from Canada who, along with his wife, daughter, and son-in-law, was returning home from travels in Europe. They were aboard *Titanic* as guests of Bruce Ismay. Hays may have chatted with another railroad man, John B. Thayer, vice president of the Pennsylvania Railroad. Thayer was aboard with his wife and their 17-year-old son, Jack. Likewise, Jacques Futrelle, a popular writer who was well known for his short stories and novels, may have conversed with Henry Sleeper Harper, a member of the family that had founded the renowned Harper & Brothers book publishing firm and a frequent traveler who was aboard with his wife.

The weather was clear but then began turning colder—a sinister sign to veteran crew members. At nine o'clock Sunday morning, April 14, an ice report came in on *Titanic*'s "wireless." This was a recent invention that allowed communication over great distances without requiring wires, unlike telegraph or telephone systems. Messages were sent in Morse code, just as they were over telegraph wires. The wireless ice report came from another vessel in the northern shipping lanes; the ship was encountering ice: large bergs, as well as smaller ones that seafarers called "growlers," and "field ice" that lay flat on the surface of the ocean. It was the first of at least six ice warnings *Titanic* would receive throughout that day and evening. (The wireless operators had received previous warnings about ice in messages Friday and Saturday.)

This ice was moving south from around the coast of Greenland. An unusually mild winter had resulted in a treacherous thaw in the arctic ice fringes. Even in more typical years, however, iceberg sightings were not at all uncommon; they were, in fact, part of the danger of North Atlantic travel. But this spring, the icebergs were more copious than usual. Veteran seafarers were uneasy.

On Sunday morning, some passengers slept, while others breakfasted late, worked out in the gym, or swam in the pool. Captain Smith led a Church of England worship service for those in first class, while a Catholic priest conducted mass for second- and third-class passengers. As they enjoyed the journey, the passengers were unaware of the crew's concerns about icebergs.

Early in the afternoon, the ship's wireless operator picked up another ice warning. This one was from *Baltic,* another White Star liner. *Titanic* had already passed areas of ice reported in earlier messages without incident. But these latest messages told of ice still awaiting *Titanic*.

Darkness brought a lovely, moonless, star-filled sky.

The sea was flat and calm. It was a cold but spectacularly beautiful evening, inspiring romantic smiles from the few bundled passengers who strolled the decks.

These conditions may have been lovely to look at, but they were far from ideal for the ship's lookouts. With no moon in sight, visibility was hampered. The falling temperature signaled the likelihood of ice not far over the horizon. The lookouts were apprehensive. Icebergs are not easily visible against a night horizon and are not always easy to recognize at a distance, especially when the sea is calm. On a turbulent sea, a sailor can see foaming breakers around an iceberg; this is not the case on a flat surface.

In his cabin on A deck, ship designer Thomas Andrews was going over charts and notebooks he'd filled with observations from the first four days of the voyage. From keel to smokestacks, Andrews knew *Titanic* far better than the captain himself did. Andrews was a managing director of Harland and Wolff, the Irish company that had built *Titanic* and other White Star liners. He was in charge of the shipbuilding company's design department. To conscientious professionals like Andrews, a shipbuilder's job was never finished. He was aboard to monitor in detail how well the ship functioned and to determine whether any adjustments might be needed. His recommendations so far ranged from major to minor. For example, he proposed to convert one end of the first-class passengers' reading and writing room into cabin space, since the reading room wasn't being used as much as he's expected. A minor change to keep in mind for future projects was the fact that too many screws had been used in the ship's hat hooks.

Nobody had any complaints about the ship's performance thus far. *Titanic* was making excellent progress. With almost two-thirds of its journey completed, the only question now among passengers and crew was whether the ship would arrive ahead of schedule.

That Sunday, White Star director Ismay enjoyed another fine dinner with the ship's doctor, listening to those seated around them singing the praises of his majestic ship. Captain Smith sat at another table that evening, smoking a second after-dinner cigar, confident everything was going smoothly. The Wideners hosted a quiet dinner party that was attended by many of the ship's most notable passengers. There was hymn singing in the second-class dining saloon.

After dinner, some passengers went to bed while others joined companions for cards and conversation. A number of men convened in the smoking room. The ship's orchestra gave a concert on A deck. Captain Smith went to the command center on the bridge at about nine o'clock. Others strolled outside. As *Titanic* forged through the middle of the North Atlantic in early spring, the air felt cold but the sky was breathtaking. One may well imagine that it was a particularly magical night for the eight newlywed couples who were spending their honeymoons on the great liner.

Seventeen-year-old Jack Thayer, recalling the clear, starry sky, later remarked, "It was the kind of night that made one feel glad to be alive."

No one knew *Titanic* better than Thomas Andrews, the man who oversaw the design and construction of the mighty ship. Andrews was onboard during *Titanic*'s maiden voyage to look for flaws that needed to be corrected, or for improvements that could be made.

Mr. and Mrs. Isidor Straus

Mr. Charles M. Hays   *Mr. Henry B. Harris*   *Mr. J. B. Thayer*

Photos of some of the rich and powerful who went down with *Titanic*, taken from a memorial book published shortly after the disaster. At the top are Isidor Straus, the owner of Macy's department store, and his wife Ida; below are (left to right) Canadian railroad baron Charles Hays, Henry B. Harris, and Pennsylvania Railroad vice president John B. Thayer.

Sometime between 9:30 and 10:00 P.M., *Titanic* received its last ice warning. The message, from the ship *Mesaba,* warned about a large ice field directly in *Titanic*'s path. However, the warning apparently was never delivered to the bridge by *Titanic*'s wireless operator, J. G. Phillips. Phillips may have thought it unnecessary to forward the message because so many other ice warnings had gone to his superiors earlier that day. Besides, he was swamped with messages to passengers that were being sent from Newfoundland on the Canadian mainland. The ship had come into Newfoundland's wireless range earlier in the evening.

The ship was slicing the smooth waters at approximately 22 knots. Just before 11:40 P.M., lookout Frederick Fleet noticed something from the crow's nest: an ominous mass, like a mountain, beginning to take shape in the near distance, directly in front of *Titanic*.

"Iceberg! Dead Ahead!"

Fleet sounded the crow's nest bell three times, then grabbed the voice phone set. There was a short delay before the bridge answered his excited call.

"What did you see?" asked the officer of the watch.

"Iceberg! Dead ahead!" Fleet reported.

First Officer William Murdoch, perhaps not believing what the watch officer reported, asked for confirmation. Fleet repeated the message.

Staring forward, Murdoch began to discern the dreaded object for himself. *Titanic* was virtually on top of it. A smaller vessel would still have had ample time to veer away, but Murdoch knew it would take

The fatal iceberg was spotted—too late—by lookout Frederick Fleet. With binoculars, Fleet might have seen the berg sooner, but there were none in *Titanic*'s lookout platform.

several minutes for a ship the size of *Titanic* to make a course change.

Why hadn't Fleet and his fellow lookout, Reginald Lee, seen the iceberg sooner? They probably would have—if they'd been using binoculars. Amazingly, *Titanic*'s lookouts had none. For some reason now unknown, the binoculars were apparently removed from the crow's nest while the ship was at Southampton.

In retrospect, the best action Murdoch could have taken would have been to reverse the engines but hold his course. A head-on collision undoubtedly would have damaged the vessel and killed some of the forward crew on duty below. But this damage would almost certainly have been confined to the first watertight compartment or two. The ship and the great majority of those aboard it would have survived. Murdoch's first instinct, however, was to try and evade the iceberg. He had little time to weigh possible damages. His only thought was to avoid a collision altogether, if possible.

Stories about his orders in the next critical moments conflict. One account says he first commanded, "Hard a-starboard!" This may have meant he wanted to veer the ship to the right. He then reportedly changed the order to "Hard a-port!": this would have switched the desired direction to the left. Might there have been a few seconds of indecision on Murdoch's part that, more than any other single factor, spelled disaster?

Don Lynch, historian for The Titanic Historical Society, explained in his 1992 book *Titanic: An Illus-*

trated History, that in traditional sailing ship navigation, Murdoch's "hard a-star-board" command would have pushed the boat's helm to starboard—which would have nosed the bow in the opposite direction. Later, ordering "hard a-port" would have swung the helm to the left, putting the ship's bow back to the right after it had passed alongside the iceberg. This combination of commands would have been an attempt to "wiggle" the ship around the berg on the port side.

However, Murdoch's exact orders are unclear. Some accounts say the first officer ordered all engines reversed simultaneously. Others say he ordered the starboard propeller full speed ahead, with the port propeller fully reversed. This counteraction of the propellers against each other would have helped turn the ship more quickly to the left than would waiting for the rudder alone to take effect. Whatever the orders, it is known that the great ship began slowly veering to port. Watching in horror as the bow bore down on the iceberg, Fleet and Lee thought the vessel would never turn.

In the final moments before impact, the rudder and propellers began to respond. The bow nosed to the left and past the ice. But the ship was not completely in the clear. The lookouts and others saw and felt the ship brush past the looming berg. Tons of ice shaved off the side of the berg tumbled onto the decks.

The collision felt like a mild tremor, or at most, a brief series of tremors. Many who had already gone to bed did not even awaken. Some of the strollers on deck

First Officer William Murdoch attempted to steer *Titanic* around the iceberg, but it took too long for the ship's bow to turn. Had Murdoch held his course, *Titanic* would probably have been severely damaged and many people would have been killed, but the liner might have stayed afloat long enough for rescue ships to arrive, allowing most of the passengers and crew to be rescued.

marveled at the giant ice mountain passing on the starboard side without realizing that the ship had actually struck it below the waterline. Oblivious to the gravity of the situation, passengers on deck began kicking chunks of ice in an impromptu soccer game. One man took some small fragments into the lounge to make a cold drink. Some of those passengers who had been sleeping felt the sensation and emerged from their cabins to ask stewards what had happened. When they noticed that the ship had stopped moving, some became concerned. But the crew did not seem worried. "There is talk of an iceberg," one woman was told. "They have stopped not to run into it."

Unbeknownst to everyone at that point—except the crewmen working on the lower decks forward—the gentle "bump" had been lethal. An underwater edge of the berg, invisible above the water, tore a long horizontal slit along *Titanic*'s starboard underside. This acted like a can opener, ripping a huge gash in the steel hull plating. Water began pouring into the forward compartments.

Taking command on the bridge, Captain Smith ordered all watertight bulkheads closed—but Murdoch had already closed them. The captain was grave as he listened to the initial reports from his officers. He sent for Thomas Andrews, the ship's builder. He wanted Andrews to go below and evaluate how extensive the damage was. Meanwhile, Smith went to the small wireless room. "We've struck an iceberg," he told operators J. G. Phillips and Harold Bride. He instructed them to be ready to send a call for help, but to wait until he received Andrews's damage report.

It didn't take Andrews long to return with dreadful

news: the ship was bound to sink! He described a tear about 200 feet long in the hull, spanning five watertight compartments along the starboard side. Water was rushing in. The water level in the first compartment was already higher than the head of a tall man. The second compartment was filling, as was the third, which was the mail room. Many of the crew working on the forward lower decks had already drowned.

Andrews explained that the bow of the ship would steadily be pulled down by inrushing water. Although the sixth compartment and those further back weren't damaged, the rising water at the bow would eventually pour over the tops of the rear bulkheads, flooding the stern compartments one by one. The watertight bulkheads would buy some time, but they could not save the ship.

Smith immediately went back to the wireless room, where Phillips had been trying to catch up with a mountain of messages between passengers and their relatives and business associates ashore. Startled by the captain's confirmation of serious damage, Phillips began transmitting an urgent call hundreds of miles in every direction: CQD MGY. ("CQD" was the international distress signal; "MGY" was *Titanic*'s call name.) The wireless operator gave the ship's position: latitude 41.46 degrees north, longitude 50.14 degrees west— about 400 miles southeast of Cape Race in Newfoundland. (Later that night, Phillips also tapped out SOS, a newer distress signal.)

By now it was 12:15 A.M., and more than 30 minutes had elapsed since the collision. As distant ships began to respond, Phillips tapped out the stark, sobering details: "We have struck an iceberg. Badly damaged.

Rush aid." The captain explained their plight to his officers and gave them instructions for evacuating the ship. Above all, he emphasized the need to remain calm. The officers knew very well that panic among more than 2,000 terrified passengers and crewmen could spell everyone's doom.

Most of the ship's crew members quickly realized that a catastrophe was about to occur. But most of the passengers initially thought the problem—whatever it was—was minor. Perhaps the ship had lost a propeller. Or perhaps it merely was stopping for the night as a precaution because of the ice reports. It was very cold. Naturally, many passengers balked at the order to appear on deck wearing lifejackets.

The first lifeboats were loaded and launched about an hour after the collision. Only a few women mustered the nerve to get inside them. They worried that they would be laughed at when they returned to the ship after the "drill" was over, chilled to the bone. Second Officer Charles Lightoller later said that at first many women "absolutely refused" to be put into the lifeboats. Others actually got back out of the boats after they'd taken seats. It still seemed much safer (not to mention more comfortable) to stay aboard the giant ship. After all, the vessel didn't seem to be sinking. They had even been reassured by stewards that they were in no danger.

As historian Logan Marshall wrote, "The heroism was that of the women who went, as well as the men who remained!" Looking down from the upper decks, it was hard to see the black surface of the water 90 feet below. But the passengers knew that the water was there—and that it was freezing. It took great courage

When *Titanic*'s sailors did begin lowering lifeboats, there were many problems. The crew had not been drilled in lifeboat procedures, lines became tangled, and the first boats were sent from the ship half-full because officers were not sure that the davits used to lower the boats could hold the weight of a full lifeboat.

for anyone, regardless of gender or age, to take to the earliest lifeboats. As a result, some of the first boats to be lowered were only partially filled. The first lifeboat, for example, carried fewer than half of the 65 passengers it could hold. Timid travelers who refused a seat in it watched from above to see what would happen to the

Margaret Brown, a wealthy passenger, took control of lifeboat number six, gaining the nickname "the unsinkable Molly Brown."

little boat dropping over the side, not yet realizing that they had forfeited a priceless opportunity for salvation.

The passengers' fear of taking to the lifeboats was reinforced by the bungling of *Titanic*'s untrained officers. After one boat settled in the water alongside the ship, its passengers looked up in horror to see another boat being lowered almost on top of it. The management of the ropes seemed to be poorly coordinated. Neither crew nor passengers had been drilled in lifeboat procedures since *Titanic* left England.

Once in the water, some of the boats were obviously lacking a designated commander. In some cases the passengers and crew members "elected" an individual to give the orders. One of the most famous of these was "the unsinkable Molly Brown." Margaret Brown, the wife of a Denver, Colorado, mining millionaire, was poorly educated, loud-mouthed, and gaudily dressed. She was also a fearless first-class passenger. As the lifeboats were being filled, Brown helped calm frightened women and youngsters and settle them into their places. Aboard lifeboat number six, she proved to be an able rower who organized other women to handle the oars. She also encouraged the shivering passengers. When the crewman in charge of the boat proved too cowardly to help rescue those in the water, she threatened to throw him overboard! Other passengers rallied behind her. Brown capably assumed command of the boat until it was picked up by a rescue ship hours later. Several survivors undoubtedly owed their lives to her.

Many heroes and heroines were made that night. Archibald Butt and John Jacob Astor, who both went down with the ship, were later called heroes by survivors. Astor and his wife both refused to enter the first lifeboat. Astor eventually placed his wife on a boat but willingly stepped back when an officer told him that no men were permitted to board. He reportedly then helped other women and children to their places as time ran out. Major Butt was credited with helping to keep order among the panicked passengers. He physically restrained men from clambering ahead of women and lifted many women and children to their seats of safety.

Another hero was Charles Joughin, the ship's chief baker. He ordered his staff to bring bread loaves on deck and distribute them among the lifeboats. Although he was assigned to command one of the boats, he refused to take a seat. He explained later that enough men already were aboard to manage the boat, and that it would have been a "bad example" for him to occupy a place while women and children remained on the sinking ship. He grabbed dozens of deck chairs and threw them into the water for swimmers to hold on. Joughin was one of the very last people to leave *Titanic*, leaping into the water from the ship's stern rail as it sank beneath the waves. Wearing a lifejacket, he was able to stay alive in the water for an amazing two hours. He was picked up by a lifeboat just before the rescue ship arrived.

Many of the luminaries aboard *Titanic* behaved well as the disaster was unfolding. Because of his old age, millionaire Isidor Straus was offered a place in a lifeboat with his wife. He refused to accept safety while women remained on the sinking ship. Mrs. Straus then vowed to stay behind with her husband. Both perished. Benjamin Guggenheim also refused the safety of a lifeboat while women and children were still on the ship. Charles Hays, Jacques Futrelle, and John Thayer helped their wives to lifeboats, but remained on the ship and perished, as did Francis David Millet. Ship designer Thomas Andrews also went down with the ship, after trying to help as many passengers to safety as he could.

The ship's musicians were among *Titanic*'s most courageous martyrs. Standing outside on the portside boat deck near the second funnel, they kept up a lively concert during the final two hours of mayhem. They poured their talent and emotion into the music, endeavoring to calm the fears of passengers—and, undoubtedly, themselves. They reportedly performed until the final minutes, going with the ship to their deaths. Among the final melodies that survivors reported hearing were the hymns "Autumn" and "Nearer My God to Thee." The lyrics of "Autumn" were especially appropriate:

Hold me up in mighty waters.
Keep my eyes on things above.

For the most part, the ship's officers worked commendably to get the lifeboats loaded and away. Second Officer Lightoller, the highest-ranking officer to survive the disaster, reportedly stood inside a boat helping load women and children. When another officer suggested he go with that boat to command it, he refused and jumped back on the sinking ship's deck. Lightoller ultimately fell into the water as the ship's upper decks slipped under. He was able to swim to an overturned boat. Taking command of the half-drowned people clinging to it, he kept it delicately balanced until the survivors were finally picked up by other lifeboats.

Steerage passengers, by and large, had few options. Some of the women were guided by stewards to the boat decks as the lifeboats were being loaded. (And like many women in first and second class, some refused to go.) But by the time most of the third-class men made their way to the upper decks, the lifeboats were away. As a result, a greater percentage of steerage passengers were lost than passengers from other classes.

As the lifeboats went over the side one by one, chaos broke out among the hundreds who remained on the listing ship's decks. Passengers fought for positions near the boat davits. Officers had to resort to force to hold back those men who fought for a precious berth in the boats amid the women and children. Most accounts agree that officers fired their pistols into the air in an attempt to maintain order; but some witnesses reported that unruly passengers seeking safety were actually shot.

Acting on rumors of lifeboat vacancies, crowds of desperate people surged from one area of the boat deck to another, from starboard to port and back, futilely

No.	Words.	Origin. Station:	Time handed in.	Via.	Remarks.
			—H.—M. / 19—		
To	*Titanic*				

One of Titanic's last wireless messages, sent by operator J. G. Phillips, used the new international distress call SOS, as well as the standard CQD.

chasing salvation. Those who fell down were trampled.

Some of the stranded passengers and crew, realizing that their chances of getting into a lifeboat were dwindling, began jumping into the icy sea. They swam out toward the lifeboats or sought out a substantial piece of floating debris—such as a crate or piece of furniture—to cling to. When they entered the freezing water, their body temperatures immediately began to plummet. A few miraculously survived an hour or two until they were picked up by lifeboats. Most, however, died in minutes.

Of *Titanic's* 24 lifeboats and collapsibles, four were wrecked during the frantic launchings. At 2:05 A.M., the last boat was lowered into the sea.

As the ship's forward angle grew steeper, one of the huge smokestacks toppled, crushing people beneath it.

Inside the ship, furniture and equipment tore loose from their moorings, screeched down the decks and crashed into columns and walls. Air hissed loudly from the remaining smokestacks. The ship's whistles shrieked at regular intervals, as if to plead for help from rescue vessels still too far away to hear.

From the wireless room Phillips continued to transmit distress signals and monitor the progress of other ships rushing to the scene. But his signal was growing weaker, and he knew the power would shut down any minute as water overtook the engine rooms below. As he and Bride worked, another crewman silently entered the wireless room and tried to steal one of the operators' lifejackets. Phillips and Bride had to knock the man unconscious. But Phillips apparently never used his life preserver: he stayed at his post until the end, frantically transmitting *Titanic*'s death knell.

Some survivors reported that First Officer Murdoch, who had been in command when the ship struck the iceberg, shot himself in the head during the final panic. Some said he first shot a male passenger who tried to take a place in a lifeboat. Others discounted the story as a rumor, probably spawned by gunshots fired by officers into the air to quell the panic. The true details of Murdoch's last moments have never been verified and remain one of many *Titanic* mysteries.

Occupants of the lifeboats weren't sure what to do after they had safely cleared *Titanic*. Looking back at the rows of shining, eerily listing lights along the ship's sides, they felt compelled to linger nearby. Perhaps they could pick up a few of the numerous swimmers thrashing in the horribly cold sea, or at least let them cling to the sides of the boats. On the other hand, many feared that desperate swimmers would swamp the boats and drag everyone to their deaths.

They were also afraid of being sucked down behind the ship when it sank. Everyone assumed that an object so large and heavy would create overpowering suction when it took its death plunge beneath the waves. The memory of the harbor incident four days earlier, when *Titanic*'s powerful wake had drawn *New York* away from its moorings and into a near-collision, was still fresh in the survivors' minds.

For those reasons, the lifeboats were rowed a quarter of a mile away or farther from the sinking *Titanic*. Survivors watched the ship's rows of lights gradually vanish below the surface. One woman described the dying ship's "tragic grandeur."

Women had to take up oars in some of the boats that carried only a few men. They found that rowing helped keep them warm. In a few instances, they handled the oars more efficiently than the cowering men in their company. "Some of the men apparently had said they could row just to get into the boats," a survivor later revealed.

As the last boat was being lowered, *Titanic*'s boiler rooms had become so flooded that Captain Smith ordered all hands on deck. They had done their duty, he told them. Now, he advised them to try to save themselves. Most of them had long since realized that for them, salvation was unlikely. But a few would defeat the icy waters and emerge alive, after all.

As with First Officer Murdoch's death, mystery surrounds Captain Smith's final minutes. According to one account, he was standing boldly on the bridge with a steward when that part of the vessel went under

As *Titanic* slipped beneath the waves, passengers in the lifeboats heard a nightmarish chorus of screams and shouts from the hundreds of people who floated in the freezing water. Because the passengers feared their small boats would be drawn under by the suction of the sinking *Titanic*, or capsized by frenzied swimmers trying to escape drowning, few of the lifeboats ventured back until it was too late. Only a handful of people were pulled alive from the icy water.

water. According to another, he dove into the ocean as the bridge was sliding under. Survivors on an overturned collapsible lifeboat recounted warning off a nearby swimmer, whom they believed may have been the captain. Those jockeying to balance on the capsized boat feared that adding one more person would overturn it. The man reportedly swam away willingly, calling back to them, "All right, boys. Good luck and God bless you." A short way off, he stopped swimming, apparently succumbing to the cold sea.

A newspaper embellished this story, publishing a sketch of the captain placing a rescued child aboard the boat, then swimming off to his death, and at least one writer later reported this alleged act of mercy as fact. However, while it is easy to imagine the captain foundering among the other swimmers as *Titanic* slipped underwater, there is no substantiated evidence that he saved a child.

The hundreds left aboard *Titanic* during its final minutes scrambled upward toward the rising stern as the ship gradually sank by the bow. They clung to railings, poles, doorknobs—anything to keep from sliding down the deck into the cold sea. Those in the surrounding lifeboats witnessed a grotesque scene: the brightly lit *Titanic* nearly perpendicular to the Atlantic, bow under water and stern raised so high that the ship's huge propellers were visible. As the angle grew steeper, the ship broke in two with a sickening crack. For a few moments the aft section settled back and leveled off somewhat. But the ocean quickly rushed into the opened compartments and tilted it almost vertically again. A terrified few made their way to the stern rail; clinging to it, they rode the stern section down into the water. Almost all of them drowned.

(Survivors who told of the ship breaking in two were doubted by the media and by investigators. It seemed incredible that such a mighty hull could tear apart. For most of the 20th century, many people assumed *Titanic* rested on the ocean floor in one piece. Only when Dr. Robert Ballard and his undersea exploration team discovered the wreck in September 1985 was the truth proven by undersea photographs. The bow and stern sections lie almost 2,000 feet apart, each surrounded by a field of debris.)

Major Arthur Peuchen, a Canadian soldier and yachtsman who because of his boating experience had been given a place in one of the lifeboats, described the ship's last moments: "I heard what seemed to be one, two, three rumbling sounds; then the lights of the ship went out. Then the terrible cries and calls for help— moaning and crying. It affected all the women in our boat whose husbands were among those in the water. This went on for some time, gradually getting fainter and fainter."

The stern rail disappeared beneath the surface at 2:20 A.M. As it turned out, the suction was much less powerful than expected as the great liner slipped under the waves. Those who had remained on the ship's after-deck until the very end found themselves struggling in the sea as the stern dropped beneath the surface. Some reported that they were within 50 or 60 feet of the vanishing hull but were not drawn under.

A few, including Second Officer Lightoller, were indeed pulled under but managed to struggle back to the surface. Lightoller reported being trapped against a grating of the ship underwater, then being blown free by an internal explosion.

Some of the passengers and crew in the lifeboats wanted to row back to help the perishing swimmers. Others were afraid to approach the scene of such mortal terror. In one boat, when some of the women urged the quartermaster in charge to turn back to the scene, he flatly refused. All they would find in the area of the sinking, he said, would be a "lot of stiffs."

The shaken survivors were a pitiful sight: young and old, mostly women and youths, some in formal evening dress, others in bedclothes. In tears, they helplessly listened to the screams for help that united across the water to make what one survivor later described as "one long, continuous moan." At the same time, they wondered whether their boats carried enough bread and water to sustain them until help arrived—or if it would come at all.

One boatload of survivors rowed several miles toward what looked like a fishing boat on the horizon in the predawn darkness. But the object—possibly a small iceberg—disappeared from sight. The disappointed passengers labored back to the scene of the sinking. In the bitter cold, some of the weaker, more poorly clad lifeboat occupants began to die of exposure. In some cases, their companions lowered their bodies over the side to make room in the boats for desperate swimmers. Those still alive and well in the boats prayed and sang, or sat in shocked silence.

Between three and four in the morning, when the last cries of the freezing swimmers had ceased and no rescue ship had yet arrived, the survivors in the boats drifted in an icy limbo. What would they do? They had no navigational charts or compasses. The nearest land—the bleak coasts of Nova Scotia and Newfound-land—was 400 miles away. New York was more than 1,200 miles away. Even if they had been closer, many of the boats had too few crewmen to navigate toward land.

The survivors couldn't ascertain from which direction a rescue ship might come. The best the numbed passengers could do was to remain in the vicinity, floating among the thickening ice, haunted by the thought of loved ones, now forever silenced by the bone-chilling sea.

News spread quickly about the disaster that had befallen *Titanic*. Although some early reports were flawed—one newspaper initially reported that all of the passengers had been rescued—the staggering scope of the disaster soon became apparent.

Rescue

In Canada and America, wireless stations began reporting fragmented details of the disaster. They were monitoring messages from other stations and from ships that had communicated with the sinking *Titanic*. The messages were short, and in many cases cryptic. It was therefore difficult to put them into any meaningful context and derive an accurate story about the unfolding drama. As a result, factually flawed accounts began filtering to the shocked public on both sides of the Atlantic on Monday morning. The Allan Line's *Virginian*, for example, was reported to have arrived at the scene and rescued *Titanic* passengers. In reality, *Virginian* was 170 miles away when it received the CQD alert; she couldn't have arrived in time to save anyone.

Dozens of other cargo and passenger ships heard *Titanic*'s call and responded. A German steamship, *Frankfurt,* was the first ship to respond to *Titanic*'s alert. Wireless operator Phillips was initially hopeful when he received a very strong replying signal from *Frankfurt*. However, the two vessels were hundreds of miles apart. By late Monday morning—*Frankfurt*'s earliest possible arrival time—even most of the survivors who'd found places in the lifeboats might be dead of exposure. And the small boats would be very difficult for any rescue ship to locate by that time, having drifted miles from the site of *Titanic*'s sinking.

Numerous other vessels picked up *Titanic*'s CQD, including *Olympic, Titanic*'s sister ship and the second-largest ocean liner in the world. *Olympic* was traveling eastward, bound for England, but was about 500 miles away and couldn't arrive any earlier than the evening of the sinking. Others that received the distress call included *Mt. Temple, Ypiranga, Birma,* and *La Provence*. Some were spacious passenger liners; others were tramp steamers. All were too far away to offer assistance.

The only ship that could come immediately to *Titanic*'s rescue was the eastbound Cunard liner *Carpathia*. This ship was estimated to be just 58 miles to the southeast, bringing a glimmer of hope to Phillips and *Titanic*'s officers. *Carpathia* was headed from New York to Gibraltar on a course south of *Titanic*'s. She received the sinking ship's emergency transmittal at 12:35 A.M. Her captain, Arthur H. Rostron, immediately changed course to assist *Titanic*.

Amazingly, another ship was very close by—some believe within 10 miles of the sinking liner. It was a small, slow steamer, stopped for the night as a safety precaution because of thickening ice in the area. She was the Leyland Line's *Californian*. Why did she never respond to *Titanic*'s calls for help and rocket flares? This question has never been answered to everyone's satisfaction.

At around 11 P.M., *Californian*'s wireless operator, Cyril Evans, had sent *Titanic* what he thought was a friendly warning: "Say, old man, we are stopped and surrounded by ice." The response from Phillips of *Titanic* had been anything but cordial: "Shut up! Shut up! I am busy." Phillips did have his hands more than full as he busily processed messages between the Cape Race station and the passengers aboard *Titanic*. *Californian* had been so close at that moment that Evans's transmittal had sounded infuriatingly loud in Phillips's headset. Phillips had been taking down a message from Cape Race when Evans interrupted. After snapping at *Californian*'s operator, Phillips apologized to the Cape Race station: "Sorry. Please repeat. Jammed."

There was little Evans could do after that but listen in on *Titanic*'s outgoing messages to shore. Businessmen sent instructions for financial transactions to their associates. Vacationers told friends or family about their glamorous holidays in Europe. Evans marveled at the staggering wealth suggested by some of those transmittals.

Because the wireless was a relatively new mode of communication, ships at sea were not required to have

Captain Arthur Rostron of the Cunard liner *Carpathia* heroically rushed to *Titanic*'s aid. *Carpathia* arrived at 4 A.M.—an hour and 40 minutes after *Titanic* sank beneath the waves—and picked up the survivors, then set out for New York.

round-the-clock service. In fact, most wireless operators were amateurs who were interested in the new technology. At 11:35 P.M., just five minutes before *Titanic*'s fateful collision with the deadly ice, Evans turned off his wireless set and went to bed. Thus, when Phillips began to tap out pleas for assistance, there was no one at *Californian*'s wireless set to hear him. *Californian*'s wireless was not back in service until the next morning.

Shortly after the collision, Captain Smith ordered flares sent up from *Titanic* at regular intervals. When *Californian*'s officers sighted flares, they woke their captain, Stanley Lord, and reported them. Without getting out of bed, Lord ordered his subordinates to try signaling the ship. When they did they could discern no answering signal from the distant vessel.

A number of *Titanic* survivors reported seeing a ship nearby at about this time. It was later widely assumed this had been *Californian*. But the problem with this conclusion was that *Titanic* eyewitnesses insisted they saw a moving vessel. Some even claimed the vessel approached within two miles, then moved away.

With a vessel in sight off the port bow and apparently headed toward them, some *Titanic* passengers were falsely reassured as they decided whether to abandon ship. They were less inclined to step into the lifeboats until they were absolutely certain that their ship was sinking because rescue seemed to be close in the form of another steamer.

The confusing reports led to speculation that a third ship was in the area, possibly moving between *Titanic* and *Californian*. Some believe the mystery ship that allegedly came within sight but vanished without communicating may have been *Samson,* a sailing ship from Norway that was illegally hunting seals off the coast of Newfoundland. Could it have been that *Titanic* and *Californian* were both in sight of *Samson*— but not of each other?

Bruce Ismay later testified before the British Board of Trade that the ship he saw from the sinking *Titanic* was in fact a sailing vessel. Asked whether he believed she was the *Californian*, he asserted, "I am sure it was not." Furthermore, *Titanic*'s flares were multicolored; those reported by *Californian*'s crew were white. Perhaps the mystery ship had responded to *Titanic*'s flares with flares of her own—the ones spotted by the *Californian*—then departed.

Whatever she was, the ship seen from *Titanic* was apparently so close that Captain Smith ordered the commanders of the first lifeboats to row to her, unload their passengers, then return for more.

But Smith's order was to no avail. It would be up to *Carpathia* to race to the tragic scene as quickly as possible. "Tell them we are coming at once with all speed," Captain Rostron of *Carpathia* instructed his wireless operator, Harold Cottam, when he learned of *Titanic*'s plight. For the next hour and a half, Cottam kept *Titanic* posted of the rescue ship's progress and solemnly recorded Phillips's worsening news: "Going down fast at the head. . . . Engine room getting flooded." At 1:50 A.M., Cottam received one last plea: "Come as quickly as possible, old man; the engine room is filling up to the boilers."

Under normal conditions, *Carpathia* averaged only 14 knots per hour. Captain Rostron pushed his ship as hard as he dared, up to 17 knots. Meanwhile, he issued orders to his crew and to the ship's doctors for receiving *Titanic* survivors. He instructed his pursers to be prepared to take the names of *Titanic* survivors for transmission to shore. Stewards were to prepare temporary bedding and dining. *Carpathia*'s passengers were instructed to remain in their cabins.

Rostron wondered whether they would arrive in time to save anyone. One of his officers saw him bow his head in silent prayer on the bridge as *Carpathia* plunged northward on its desperate mission.

Carpathia arrived at the ice-infested disaster scene at 4 A.M.—having made astonishingly good time. For the final hour of its race, the rescue ship had fired rockets every 15 minutes, hoping to assure *Titanic* survivors of her imminent approach. Even after encountering icebergs himself, Rostron maintained full speed, striving desperately to reach *Titanic*. By 3:35 he realized that if *Titanic* was still floating, his lookouts would have sighted it on the horizon. Hope waned.

As sunrise gradually began to light the scene, shivering survivors saw *Carpathia* stopped in the water. All were amazed to see just how treacherous the sea had become. Masses of ice stretched for miles. Icebergs floated menacingly on every side. A *Carpathia* officer counted 25 bergs more than 250 feet tall and dozens of others large enough to cause damage.

One by one, for the next four hours the lifeboats and collapsibles drew alongside *Carpathia*. They held women who had lost husbands; exhausted crewmen; men who had traded their honor for a place in a lifeboat; a nurse holding a baby whose parents were both lost; a woman traveling second class who had been saved with three of her children while her husband and seven other children drowned; two parentless French boys, aged two and four, who couldn't tell rescuers where they were from or where they were going. All were dazed and numb from the cold.

The weary, freezing passengers were of little help to their rescuers. They climbed up rope ladders or were hoisted up in slings. For many of the exhausted survivors, this was a final terrifying moment to conclude their night of constant terror. One woman later said that the most frightening part of the whole ordeal was not the sinking of *Titanic* or the uncertain hours at sea in an open boat, but being lifted aboard *Carpathia*.

Carpathia's passengers were stunned at the sight of ocean travelers just like themselves who, in one unexpected moment, had been taken to the brink of death. That it had happened aboard the awesome *Titanic* made the entire spectacle even more shocking. Sympathetic *Carpathia* passengers needed little prompting to open their cabins and provide clothing to the victims, who had lost everything. *Carpathia* crewmen gave their sleeping berths to their *Titanic* counterparts. Even more importantly, their words and gestures comforted hundreds who had just lost spouses, children, and parents. In *Carpathia*'s main dining room, the chaplain held a special memorial service for those lost at sea.

Californian finally drew near at about eight o'clock that morning. By then *Carpathia* was ready to depart for New York with the 705 survivors its crew had taken from the water. More than 1,500 lives had been lost. Other rescue ships arrived and searched the area for additional survivors. They found none. Over the next few days they pulled some 300 corpses from the water, scattered over a surface area of more than 100 miles. (One decomposed body was recovered by a transatlantic steamer two months after the sinking. It, like many of those found earlier, was buried at sea.) Satisfied they had done all they could, the rescue captains cautiously picked their way out of the ice field. They left behind them, two and a half miles beneath the waves, the remains of what had been the world's greatest ship, broken in two on the frigid ocean floor.

Naturally, the survivors aboard the now-crowded *Carpathia* were desperate for word of missing loved ones. Early rumors suggested many they'd left behind on the sinking *Titanic* had been rescued by other ships. *Titanic* passengers swarmed the wireless room, dispatching inquiries about specific individuals and sending word of their own safety to relatives in America and England.

On shore, newspapers began reporting wild stories about the disaster that were based on pieces of intercepted wireless transmittals as well as outright rumors. "All Saved from the *Titanic* after Collision," the *Evening Sun* in New York assured readers in a banner headline.

By Monday night, however, the truth was known: two-thirds of those aboard *Titanic* had perished. Only *Carpathia* had found any survivors. Aboard the rescue ship, *Titanic* victims had only each other to ask for any information about their lost relatives' final moments.

In addition to loved ones, many of the survivors had also lost their fortunes. Poor immigrants who had been traveling to America in steerage were especially hard hit by the loss of every possession they owned.

Many of those rescued were injured or sick from

their ordeal. *Carpathia*'s dining rooms became hospitals or temporary sleeping quarters. The injured included *Titanic* wireless operator Harold Bride. His frostbitten feet bound in bandages, Bride had to be carried off *Carpathia* when she arrived in New York three days later.

White Star Line officials at first considered transferring the survivors from *Carpathia* to the more spacious *Olympic*, *Titanic*'s sister ship. But many of the survivors objected to the very idea of another midocean transfer from ship to boat to ship. It was a difficult and not altogether safe procedure. In the end Captain Rostron and Bruce Ismay—who had survived aboard

Titanic survivors huddle on the deck of *Carpathia* as the ship enters New York harbor.

As word began to spread about *Titanic*'s sinking, anxious crowds gathered, waiting for news.

one of *Titanic*'s lifeboats—agreed that it would be best for *Carpathia* to take the survivors directly to their original destination: New York. Ismay, severely depressed, retreated to a cabin and remained in seclusion until *Carpathia* docked.

New Yorkers greeted the survivors of the *Titanic* tragedy with open arms. Hospitals made whole wards available for those disembarking from *Carpathia* who might need medical attention. City officials made every possible arrangement for their comfort and well-being. Police were diverted to the harbor to manage the throngs of spectators. Doctors, nurses, and ambulances from every downtown hospital—and from outside the city—were at dockside. Private citizens opened their homes and hosted survivors for as long as they needed shelter. A variety of public, private, and church-related shelters prepared for an influx of *Titanic* passengers.

Wealthy citizens dispatched limousines to the Cunard pier to transport survivors to waiting shelters. A delegation from the New York Stock Exchange brought a box of cash for distribution among the steerage passengers. The directors of the American Red Cross, the Salvation Army, and other relief organizations met *Carpathia* at the pier in person. The Pennsylvania Railroad offered free transportation to any *Titanic* survivor who wanted to go west. Government officials agreed not to require immigrants from *Titanic* to register at Ellis Island, the legal entry point for immigrants arriving in New York. Instead, immigration inspectors were assigned to the Cunard offices and ordered to complete the paperwork for the beleaguered arrivals as quickly as possible.

Also waiting on the pier for *Carpathia* Thursday night were about 2,000 somber relatives and friends. It was estimated that a total of more than 30,000 people stood along the waterfront, weathering a cold rain to glimpse the rescue ship and its tragic human cargo. Millionaires and poor working-class relatives stood silently together, united in grief. Some were there hoping to meet lost loved ones, refusing to believe they could have drowned.

Captain Rostron had wired lists of survivors' names to New York, but he had refused to reply to queries from the press. He wanted to protect the victims from

Titanic's lifeboats were carried to New York by *Carpathia* and released to White Star Line officials. The lifeboats then disappeared, and no one is certain what happened to them.

a blitz of publicity and leave them in peace to cope with their losses. Rostron knew he would be criticized for his silence during *Carpathia*'s sad return to New York, but he was more concerned about minimizing the stress of the survivors. "I gave instructions to send first all official messages, then names of passengers, then survivors' private messages," he later stated. Rostron also noted that communications were hampered by the poor condition of his ship's wireless set and by constant interruptions from both ship and shore wireless operators.

When *Carpathia* entered the harbor Thursday evening, tugs and other boats nosed alongside. Reporters shouted questions to passengers who peered down from *Carpathia*'s rails. "Were the women properly cared for after the crash?" "Is it true that some of the lifeboats sank with the *Titanic*?" "Is Mr. John Jacob Astor on board?"

The passengers could barely hear the questions and, even when they did hear, they did not know all the answers. They shouted back statements and questions of their own that were misunderstood or drowned out by the noise of the engines and the cacophony of voices. The result was continued frustration for the media and officials who had been waiting since Monday for accurate details of the disaster. Some accused Captain Rostron of conspiring with the White Star Line to cover up the facts. Information was coming much too slowly to satisfy a waiting, disbelieving world.

Even if clearer communication had been possible, reporters would have gotten an inaccurate picture of the sinking. The survivors simply couldn't keep track of all the details. (For example, one woman told reporters *Titanic* struck the iceberg at 9:45—two hours before the collision actually occurred.) It would be up to official inquiries to sort through hundreds of conflicting accounts in order to reconstruct the tragedy.

As *Carpathia* approached its berth, it released *Titanic*'s lifeboats into the custody of White Star officials. Observers fell silent. Here was the first hard, undeniable evidence that the world's greatest ship, which until four days earlier had proudly ruled the waves, was no more.

Placing the Blame, or Making Excuses?

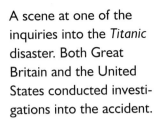

The question on everyone's mind after the sinking of *Titanic* was, "Why did it happen?" How could the largest, safest ship ever built sink so quickly because of just one iceberg—on a clear night in a glassy, calm sea? And why were so few of its occupants saved? It was too baffling for anyone to comprehend. To this day, although volumes of research have been devoted to the topic, many students of *Titanic* history aren't fully satisfied with the answers.

Sorting out the evidence and conflicting testimony was no easy task. Rumors and accusations were flying before the survivors were even brought ashore; charges would continue for years to come. A stoker from the ship's engine room claimed that a fire was smoldering in one

The White Star Line's Bruce Ismay (right), who survived the sinking, was photographed on his way to testify at the U.S. Senate's *Titanic* inquiry. With Ismay are his wife Florence and fellow White Star director Harold Sanderson.

of the coal bunkers from the time *Titanic* left England. If the stoker's claim was true, might that fire have contributed to the disaster?

A passenger whose cabin was directly above the engines reported that as he read in his bed before retiring that Sunday night, he felt unusually strong vibrations from the great machinery below. Did the increased vibrations indicate that *Titanic* was steaming faster than ever—on a night when icebergs had been sighted in the area by other ships?

Another survivor reported being in a lifeboat with two lookouts and overhearing them complain that their iceberg alarm had been directed to the bridge a full 15 minutes before the collision, only to be ignored by the officer on the bridge until it was too late. The question of recklessness on Captain Smith's part was immediately raised and has never been completely resolved.

Were the officers using pistols to control men who were jostling to overrun the lifeboats, as some survivors reported? If so, was anyone actually shot? And what of the reports of a mysterious ship that passed within a mile or two of *Titanic* as she sank but went away without helping?

The job of sifting through *Titanic* information—and misinformation—was assumed by two groups of investigators, one in America and one in England. A U.S. Senate subcommittee immediately began an inquiry. The American examination was followed by an official investigation by the British Board of Trade as the principal figures involved in the tragedy began returning to England. The two investigations were quite different. Each one was later criticized, but both turned up helpful findings.

Shortly after *Carpathia* docked in New York Harbor, U.S. senators William Alden Smith of Michigan and Francis Newlands of Nevada came aboard. They served Bruce Ismay with a subpoena. It ordered Ismay to appear at a Senate subcommittee inquiry, headed by Smith, before he returned to England.

Senator Smith was afraid that many of the passengers and crew would leave New York before they could be questioned. So he opened his inquiry the very morning after *Carpathia* docked, holding it at the famous Waldorf-Astoria Hotel. Ismay was the first witness called to testify.

Britons were angered by the impromptu American investigation because *Titanic* was a British vessel. Despite Senator Smith's justification—that an American inquiry was in order because so many of the ship's passengers had been Americans—most people in England still believed that the only official inquiry should be conducted by the British Board of Trade.

As the Senate questioning proceeded during the following weeks, Britons derided the nautical ignorance of Smith and the other American senators. At one point, for example, Smith asked a *Titanic* officer where icebergs come from. The witness gave the sarcastic response, "As far as I understand, they come from the Arctic region."

Key witnesses besides Ismay included Second Officer Charles Lightoller, wireless operator Harold Bride, and *Californian*'s captain, Stanley Lord.

For Ismay, the two main areas of questioning concerned whether he'd prompted Captain Smith to push the ship to unsafe speeds and how he'd found a place in a lifeboat when so many women passengers were left behind. Asked point blank whether he ever urged Captain Smith to go faster, Ismay replied, "No, sir."

During another appearance before the committee, Ismay was asked about his being aboard a lifeboat. He snapped, "The boat was there. There was a certain number of men in the boat, and the officer called out asking if there were any more women, and there was no response, and there were no passengers left on the deck." He said he stepped in "as the boat was in the act of being lowered away." What about the shortage of lifeboats on *Titanic*? Ismay pointed out that the ship "had sufficient boats to obtain her passenger certificate [from the British Board of Trade]."

Lightoller, by all accounts, had performed admirably during the frantic loading of the lifeboats and the subsequent hours adrift waiting for *Carpathia*. When questioned, he seemed determined to defend his company. At one point, he was asked, "Did you know you were in the vicinity of icebergs [during the hours before the collision]?" Amazingly, Lightoller responded, "No, sir." Upon further questioning, however, he had to admit that he had discussed the ice-related warnings with Captain Smith that Sunday afternoon.

Captain Lord of *Californian* testified that the ship he and his crew saw in the middle of the night was clearly too small to have been the superliner *Titanic*. Various testimony by his officers further strengthened the theory that a third ship had been in the area. For example, one *Californian* officer said the rockets he saw seemed to have come up from the horizon on the other side of the nearby ship. *Californian* officers also gave conflicting reports as to whether the ship they saw was listing or whether it was steaming away from them.

After the Senate committee finished its investigation in May, Smith reported to the full Senate. He cited a combination of reasons for *Titanic*'s sinking and for the heavy casualties.

Second Officer Charles Lightoller, the highest-ranking *Titanic* officer to survive, was a key witness in both the British and U.S. inquiries. Lightoller oversaw the lifeboat loading and saved numerous passengers. When the ship went under, he swam to an overturned boat and helped others out of the water, directing them to keep the upside-down lifeboat afloat until the other boats could pick up the survivors.

First, he judged that Captain Smith had been over-confident in his ship's indestructibility. For that reason the captain had not been sufficiently concerned about the ice warnings he had received all day and evening on the Sunday of the collision. As for the ship's speed, the senator believed that the captain had not experienced direct pressure from White Star officials to reach New York sooner than expected. However, he did suggest that the mere presence of Bruce Ismay and Thomas Andrews on *Titanic* tacitly encouraged the captain to push the ship as fast as he dared.

Second, when the order was given to abandon ship, it was not carried out well. Some of the crew failed to report to their emergency stations at all. Those who loaded some of the lifeboats were in such a rush that they lowered them and sent them away with many precious seats unoccupied. Senator Smith remarked that "nearly 500 people were needlessly sacrificed for want of orderly discipline in loading." Once at sea, some of the boat crews pulled away to a safe distance and refused to return to rescue others, even though they had room for more survivors.

Third, the crew seemed relatively indifferent to the plight of the steerage passengers. By the time travelers from the lower decks made their way up, most of the lifeboats were gone.

Fourth, wireless policies were woefully lax. If shipping companies had required wireless devices to be in operation day and night, the nearby *Californian* would have been alerted and could have saved most of *Titanic*'s passengers and crew.

Fifth, the captain of *Californian* should have responded to *Titanic*'s signal flares. Senator Smith concluded that *Californian* had been within 20 miles of the sinking ship and should have come to investigate.

Senator Smith pointed out another safety deficiency revealed by the inquiry, although mercifully it caused no further loss of life that night. The lifeboats were poorly equipped. Only three had lamps; none contained a compass! Had *Carpathia* not arrived as quickly as it did, the chance of rescue would have grown increasingly slim for the wretched survivors as the morning progressed. As it had turned out, some of the boats were already scattered over several miles of ocean.

The Senate committee also issued a list of recommended remedies:

- Ships should carry enough lifeboats for everyone aboard, and regular boat drills should be held.
- All ships carrying more than 100 passengers should have two searchlights.
- Every passenger liner should have a wireless set, with operators on duty round-the-clock. And the use of wireless equipment should be regulated to prevent "hams" (amateurs) from interfering during a crisis.
- The design of watertight bulkheads and decks should be improved.

The committee also recommended that U.S. shipping inspectors stop waiving the lower safety standards of ships from certain foreign countries. The reason for this recommendation was that ships that called at American ports and carried American passengers should follow American safety regulations.

The rumor that the ship's coal supply had been on fire throughout the voyage was apparently brushed aside. If there was in fact a fire, it was not thought to have played a role in the sinking.

*   *   *

Americans were even more scornful of the British investigation than Britons had been of Senator Smith's. In the minds of many historians, the inquiry in London was little more than a "whitewash." After all, the British Board of Trade that conducted it was the same government agency that had proclaimed *Titanic*'s number of lifeboats sufficient. The inquiry was presided over by Lord Mersey, Sir John Charles Bigham. It began about three weeks after the sinking. The U.S. probe had not been completed yet, and some of the key witnesses were still in America.

Second Officer Lightoller testified for a day and a half in London. He strongly defended the actions of Captain Smith both before and after the collision. When asked about *Titanic*'s speed in the face of ice warnings, Lightoller insisted that it had not been unusually fast. In his years of North Atlantic crossings, he testified, "I have never seen the speed reduced" under circumstances like those under which *Titanic* steamed that night. When a questioner suggested that the ship's speed was reckless for the icy conditions, Lightoller retorted, "Then all I can say is that reckless-ness applies to practically every commander and every ship crossing the Atlantic Ocean."

Did he believe that *Titanic*'s officers were practicing "careful navigation" that night?

"It is ordinary navigation," Lightoller said, "which embodies careful navigation."

The second officer could not deny shortcomings in

the way the ship was evacuated, however. The passengers had not been drilled in lifeboat procedures. Lightoller told the Board of Inquiry that a passenger drill had been scheduled for Sunday, the day of the collision, but had never been carried out.

In the end the British board formally declared Captain Smith and his officers innocent of negligence. It also ruled that J. Bruce Ismay's behavior was not cowardly. Ismay and another man had entered one of the last collapsible boats just before it was lowered. Minutes earlier, other men had been warned away by an officer's pistol when they tried to board that lifeboat. Many observers saw this as evidence that Ismay was given a special privilege on the boat deck. On the other hand, survivors also reported seeing Ismay helping women and families into the first boats to leave. Some historians think he merely took a seat in a partly filled lifeboat and didn't intentionally take the place of any women or children. Considering the confusion of the moment, it was hard to reconstruct the exact circumstances under which Ismay took to the boat. Regardless, he lived the rest of his life disgraced in the eyes of many.

Lord Mersey concluded that steerage passengers on *Titanic* had been treated fairly as the lifeboats were lowered. But the survival of a number of the men from first class—such as Sir Cosmo Duff-Gordon, whose lifeboat built for more than 40 people rowed away from the ship bearing just 12—as well as the glaring disparity in survival statistics between the classes prompted an irate public outcry:

- In first class, 31 percent of the men were saved, and 93 percent of the women and children.

Messrs Coutts Bank Ltd.
Strand. London. W.C

April 16th 12.

Pay to J. Horswell.   or order.

The sum of. Five Pounds,

£5. 0. 0.

Cosmo Duff Gordon

During the *Titanic* inquiry, rumors circulated that Sir Cosmo Duff-Gordon had paid the crewmen manning his lifeboat not to return and pick up swimmers after the liner sank. This copy of a check for £5 from Duff-Gordon to one of the crew members was exhibited during the inquiry. Although Sir Cosmo and Lady Duff-Gordon defended their actions until their deaths in the 1930s, their reputations were ruined.

- In second class, 11 percent of the men survived, and 81 percent of the women and children.
- In third class, 14 percent of the men and only 47 percent of the women and children survived.

Only 214 of the 890 crew members were saved.

Titanic historians have acknowledged that although the lifeboat shortage seems appalling today, travelers at the time knew full well that ocean liners carried insufficient lifeboats. Until *Titanic*'s loss, the issue was rarely debated or challenged in the media or by regulatory bodies.

Logan Marshall, who wrote the first book about the disaster shortly after it occurred, lamented, "It is heartrending to stop and think that thirty-two more life-boats, costing only about $16,000, which could have been stowed away without being noticed on the broad decks of *Titanic*, would have saved every man, woman and child on the steamer. There has never been so great a disaster in the history of civilization due to the neglect of so small an expenditure."

Stowing three times more lifeboats in easy-to-launch places would not actually have been as simple as Marshall implied. But few questioned the notion that every traveler was entitled to a guaranteed place in a lifeboat. Marshall suggested that the White Star Line didn't skimp on lifeboats in order to cut costs. Instead, the goal was to give passengers more room to enjoy the promenade deck—another sign of a luxury-first, safety-second mentality.

Today historians generally agree that four factors contributed to the *Titanic* calamity:

- Flawed design and insufficient safety equipment. *Titanic*'s watertight bulkheads did not extend high enough from the keel. There were too few lifeboats and searchlights.
- Lack of crew discipline and safety training. The crew of *Titanic* was by no means a well-rehearsed "team." This problem stemmed primarily from last-minute crew additions the White Star Line made in Southampton. Because of a coal strike, the company had postponed the departures of some of its other vessels and transferred their coal to *Titanic* for its maiden voyage. Some of those ships' passengers had been rebooked aboard *Titanic*. Some of their crew members were also reassigned—to a huge ship with which they were unfamiliar. The crew wasn't adequately trained in lowering *Titanic*'s

lifeboats. The passengers had not been drilled in their use, either.

- Conditions at sea. The flat calm surface meant that there were no breakers to indicate the presence of icebergs, and there was no moonlight.
- Carelessness. Although *Titanic*'s speed might have been considered typical by shipping officials of the day, the vessel was obviously moving too fast to avoid the iceberg after it was sighted.

Numerous shortcomings and tragic ironies came to light during the hearings. None of them alone was enough to cause the disaster, but taken together, they contributed to the heavy loss of life. For example, it has been pointed out that *Titanic*'s most efficient pumps were placed in the engine room. This was a logical design, but it meant that those pumps were practically worthless in the *Titanic* disaster. Had they been located in a forward compartment, they might have helped keep the ship afloat a few precious minutes longer.

The inquiry panels in both America and England treated Captain Lord of *Californian* harshly. They thought he'd had ample evidence that a nearby ship was in distress, but he'd elected to do nothing to help.

Lord Mersey concluded that *Californian* had been within 10 miles of *Titanic*, or half the distance estimated in the U.S. Senate report. "Had she [gone to *Titanic*'s assistance] she might have saved many if not all of the lives that were lost," he determined.

Historian Walter Lord (no relation) speculates that *Californian*'s captain may have chosen to ignore the rocket flares out of "undue caution." Fearing the ice floes, he had interrupted his own voyage for the night.

Not sure what the flares were all about, he wasn't willing to endanger his ship to investigate. Had he realized *Titanic* was in distress, he unquestionably would have responded, according to Walter Lord. To this day, however, most people who read about *Titanic* are left with a scornful impression of *Californian*'s captain. He has frequently been branded as "negligent" for ignoring what were obviously distress signals.

The Leyland Line pressured Captain Lord to resign his command after the inquiries. He was fortunate enough to sign with another shipping company within six months of his resignation. He served many more years as a sea captain with no further incidents tarnishing his record.

Stanley Lord, captain of the liner *Californian*, was harshly criticized by both the British and U.S. inquiry boards for not going to *Titanic*'s aid. *Californian* was less than 20 miles from *Titanic* when the ship hit the iceberg.

Second Officer Lightoller was kept on by the White Star Line. But he soon realized the company was not happy with his presence, as he was a reminder of its darkest hour. It was unlikely that the line ever would offer him a significant promotion, so Lightoller retired from service. During the early months of World War II, more than 25 years after the *Titanic* disaster, Lightoller crossed the English Channel in his yacht, *Sundowner,* to aid in the daring civilian rescue of the British Army pinned on the shore at Dunkirk.

Frederick Fleet, the lookout who reported the iceberg to *Titanic*'s bridge, survived the sinking and served aboard ships for two more decades. He spent his later years working as a night watchman, then selling newspapers on the street. He committed suicide in 1965.

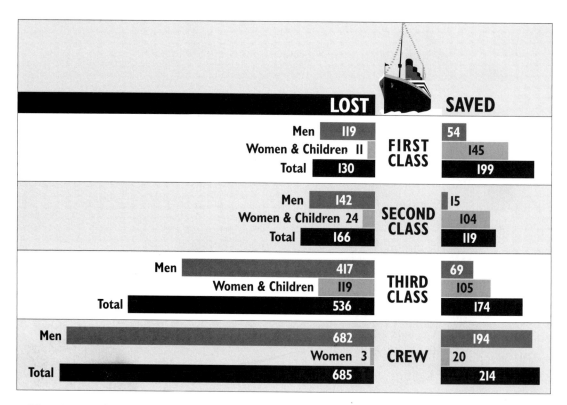

	LOST		SAVED
FIRST CLASS			
Men	119	54	
Women & Children	11	145	
Total	130	199	
SECOND CLASS			
Men	142	15	
Women & Children	24	104	
Total	166	119	
THIRD CLASS			
Men	417	69	
Women & Children	119	105	
Total	536	174	
CREW			
Men	682	194	
Women	3	20	
Total	685	214	

This chart shows the disparity between *Titanic*'s classes. In third class, more women and children were lost (119) than were saved (105). By contrast, just 11 of 156 women and children traveling first class died in the sinking.

Captain Arthur Rostron of *Carpathia* has been remembered as an undisputed hero. Journalists of the day criticized him for thwarting their attempts to question passengers as the rescue ship arrived in New York. But fittingly, Rostron was knighted and became commodore of the Cunard Line.

Captain Smith will always remain something of an enigma. To some he was clearly reckless, driving the ship too fast in the face of ice warnings. To others he was practical and conservative to the end. *Titanic*'s third officer, Herbert Pitman, testified that more than six hours before the collision, Smith had ordered the ship to take a course slightly south of the scheduled route. Presumably Smith's alteration of the route was prompted by the ice reports. Furthermore, ships often steamed at full speed through icy waters. Captains expected their lookouts to spot any dangerous icebergs in plenty of time to steer clear of them.

The related question—whether Smith was pressured by Ismay to arrive early in New York—will probably remain unanswered. While many nautical experts insist that a veteran captain could never have been persuaded to jeopardize his ship's safety in order to post a faster speed, some *Titanic* passengers insisted otherwise. One, Elizabeth Lines of New York, reported overhearing a luncheon conversation between Ismay and Smith, who were seated near her table. Ismay seemed pleased with the ship's progress, she recalled, but told the captain plainly, "We will make a better run tomorrow. . . . We will beat the *Olympic* and get in to New York on Tuesday."

Another passenger, Mrs. Emily Ryerson, later reported a conversation she had with Ismay while lounging with a friend on deck late that fateful Sunday afternoon. Ismay allegedly told them that the ship was traveling at about 20 to 21 knots, and added, "We are going to start up some new boilers this evening." The implication was that he wanted the ship to increase its speed.

What is certain is that in the end, Captain Smith, in the noblest tradition of seafarers, was lost with his ship. A bronze statue of him can be seen in his hometown of Lichfield, England.

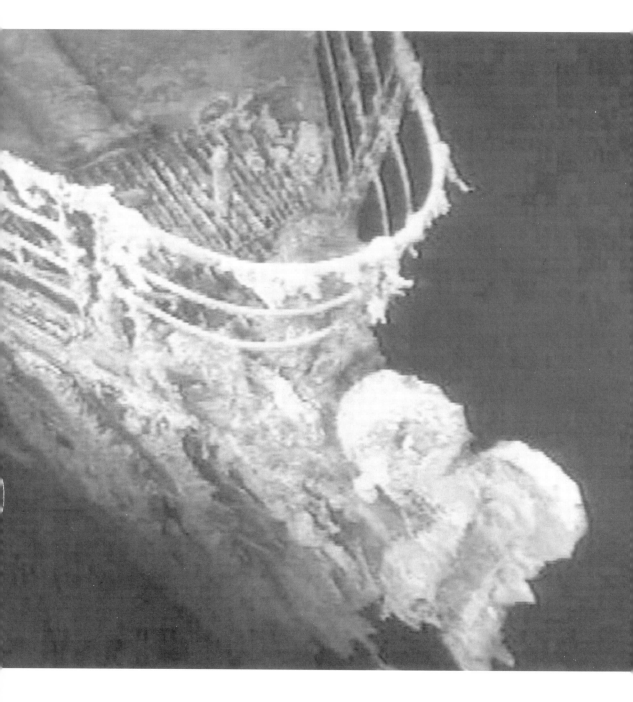

This view of the submerged prow of *Titanic* was captured on videotape. The exact location of *Titanic*'s remains was unknown until 1985, when Dr. Robert Ballard led an undersea exploration that found the wreckage.

A Safer Ocean

Within weeks of *Titanic*'s sinking—even before the U.S. Senate committee made its report in May—shipping companies began instituting changes to prevent another such calamity in the future. The International Mercantile Marine announced that all its ships would be required to carry enough lifeboats or rafts for every passenger and crew member, even though some countries' shipping regulations were still less demanding.

Some improvements were obvious and immediate; others stemmed from long-term policies. North Atlantic shipping lanes were altered. By directing vessels to cross the ocean farther south, shipping companies lessened the risk of encountering killer icebergs. In fact, the day after

Titanic sank, the shipping lane it had followed was shifted approximately 60 miles southward. This meant the passenger lines, after years of arguably reckless competition, were forced to ensure safety first. A more southerly course, they knew, would add a few hours to their ships' travels between England and America.

How could this be? On a flat map, the new routes appeared to be a straighter line between the two continents. Remember, however, that the earth is round. What looks like a northerly arc on a flat map becomes the most direct "straight line" when the map is plotted on a round globe. "The shortest course between New York and the English Channel lies across Nova Scotia and Newfoundland," Captain William S. Sims, a U.S. Navy officer, commented after the sinking. "Consequently, the shortest water route is over seas where navigation is dangerous by reason of fog and ice. It is a notorious fact that the transatlantic steamships are not navigated with due regard to safety, that they steam at practically full speed in the densest fogs."

Sims defended shipping companies, however. He said they were merely complying with public demand. If certain ships were known to take longer routes around the ice and to slow down in foggy weather, many customers would book passage on competing vessels with a reputation for making the best crossing time, regardless of the risks.

Pressure mounted quickly for adequate lifeboats aboard every ship. J. Bruce Ismay, the disgraced White Star official who survived the sinking, acknowledged that every soul aboard a ship should be guaranteed a place in a lifeboat in the event of an emergency. Logan Marshall, in his book about the disaster, noted, "If life-boats for one-third of those on the ship are necessary, life-boats for all on board are equally necessary." Marshall noted the irony of the luxury liner's design: *Titanic* offered pleasure facilities never before seen on a ship, but a woefully inadequate number of lifeboats. "These [lifeboats] would seem more important than fireplaces, squash courts, and many other luxuries with which the *Titanic* was provided," wrote Marshall.

This thinking differed from the outdated policies of shipping regulators. Until the *Titanic* tragedy, lifeboats were never expected to be able to take away all persons aboard a ship in distress.

Senator Smith, who chaired the American committee investigating the *Titanic* disaster, introduced a bill calling for wide-ranging reforms in shipping practices. He believed a ship should not only have ample lifeboats but also each passenger and crew member should be assigned a specific place in a boat. Smith's bill also called for a minimum number of trained crew to handle each lifeboat.

Government boats began to patrol the North Atlantic shipping lanes to check for ice. Two U.S. Navy cruisers were soon stationed on the Grand Banks. This early effort to monitor ocean ice during the spring months led to the creation of the International Ice Patrol in 1914. It was endorsed by 13 countries.

Ships that found themselves near dangerous ice fields at nightfall were required to reduce speed and/or change course.

Communication was also improved. It was clear to everyone that if the wireless operator aboard the nearby *Californian* had been on duty for at least part of the night, he would have picked up *Titanic*'s distress

Harold Bride, one of *Titanic*'s two wireless operators, works in the liner's wireless room. (The photographer accidentaly double-exposed the image, which was made before the ship left England.) Following the *Titanic* disaster, ships were required to have round-the-clock wireless—and later radio—service.

signals. Wireless apparatus wasn't common on smaller ships of the day, or on older passenger ships that catered mainly to immigrants and working-class travelers. In 1912 wireless was still something of a novelty. It was developed for the convenience of passengers who wanted to communicate with parties on shore while at sea. In fact the wireless operators aboard *Titanic* were not employed by the White Star Line; they were contractors placed there by Marconi's Wireless Telegraph Company to process messages for paying passengers.

Senator Smith's bill called not only for 24-hour wireless operation but also for each ship's wireless set to have a range of at least 100 miles. And those wireless sets had to have auxiliary power, so that they were not dependent solely on the ship's engines (which might fail soon after a ship began to sink). Smith also urged that wireless sets be required on all ships carrying more than 50 passengers. Not surprisingly, stock in the Marconi Company skyrocketed in the days following the disaster.

In addition, SOS became the new standard distress signal. Until the *Titanic* tragedy, wireless operators rarely sent it, preferring the established CQD. But SOS, immortalized by *Titanic*'s operators, caught on partly because it was quicker to transmit in the chaos of an emergency, and easy for telegraph operators to recognize in Morse code: three dots, three dashes, three dots.

In response to the inaction of *Californian*, Senator Smith demanded that the use of rocket flares be reserved only for emergencies. Previously, signal flares might go up amid the gaiety of a shipboard party. Smith proposed that the use of rockets for anything but emergency signaling be a punishable misdemeanor.

As the 20th century progressed, nautical communication and navigational aids became increasingly sophisticated. All ships were equipped with wireless sets, and eventually with voice radio sets. Radar could detect and outline distant ships and other objects, giving captains minutes or even hours of advance warning that their vessels were on potential collision courses. Pinpointing a ship's exact position on the vast sea became a precision science with the introduction of long-range navigation (loran), a type of radio device. Today satellite technology adds a new dimension of safety to oceanic navigation.

Of course these improvements did not come about just because of the *Titanic* disaster. But the enormous and lasting impression made by the events of April 14–15, 1912, more than any other single factor, demonstrated the urgent need for better communication at sea.

The inquiries in America and England brought to light the sad fact that *Titanic*'s crew and passengers were not prepared for any sort of emergency—much less a fatal encounter with an iceberg. *Titanic*'s survivors, in a resolution drawn up after the disaster, pointed out that "stokers, stewards, etc., are not efficient boat handlers." As a result of subsequent changes in the 20th century, ship crews are now thoroughly trained in lifesaving procedures. There still is no guarantee that a lifeboat adrift on the open ocean will be found, especially if it floats aimlessly for many days. But passengers today at least stand an excellent chance of safely leaving a sinking ship and finding a place in a boat or raft. Senator Smith's bill called for mandatory lifeboat drills for both crew and passengers.

Ships must now undergo rigorous testing. Before they can finalize a contract, shipbuilders must meet the requirements not only of the shipping company but also of the government. A vessel must meet strict standards—tougher than most emergencies will require. Inspectors examine in detail a ship's fittings and other construction material and make sure everything operates as it should.

In the long run, perhaps the most positive result of this horrible disaster may have been a marked change in attitude. During the Edwardian era (the period beginning in 1908 when Edward VII became king of England), people in Europe and America lived by an unspoken code of strict class distinctions. Rich aristocrats refused to mingle in any way with the working class. The poor accepted it as their lot to have the leftovers in life. The first and the best of everything, they

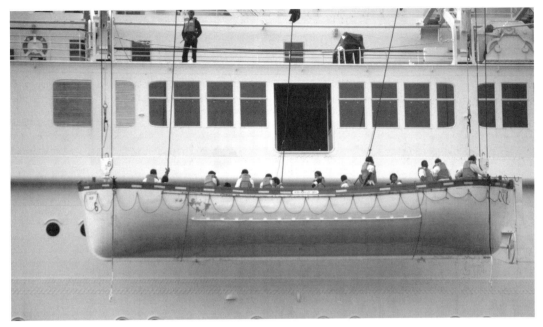

knew, went automatically to the wealthy. This Edwardian mind-set is believed to have been one reason for the heavy losses among *Titanic*'s steerage passengers. Both during the voyage and during the panic as the lifeboats were loaded and lowered, many of *Titanic*'s crew tended to give preferential treatment to the highest-paying passengers. Some of the wealthy travelers assumed that they were entitled to have first chance at the boats. They reasoned that their hefty ticket prices also bought them the right to extra safety and security.

The lot of ordinary seamen didn't improve dramatically, or rapidly, however. Crew members on even a prestigious liner such as *Titanic* were woefully underpaid. Those who found refuge on *Carpathia* knew that the White Star Line would refuse to replace their lost clothing and possessions—and would dock their pay from the time the ship went down!

Today, passengers and crew members of cruise ships are required to participate in lifeboat drills, to eliminate the chaos and confusion that characterized the launching of *Titanic*'s lifeboats. And unlike *Titanic*, ships today must have enough lifeboats to carry everyone aboard.

(continued on p. 108)

OTHER FAMOUS SHIPWRECKS

Although maritime safety improved even as the era of ocean liners waned, sea tragedies didn't cease altogether. Melvin Maddocks, a historian who studies ocean liners, observed that despite watertight bulkheads, double bottoms, and other safety precautions that came about early in the 20th century, the great vessels "remained as vulnerable as the men who rode their bridges." There have been many well-known disasters at sea in the years since the sinking of *Titanic*, although none approach the level of her mystique or interest. The following stories illustrate some of the enduring hazards of water transport:

- *Lusitania.* Wartime poses increased maritime hazards, even to the ships of neutral countries. This glorious Cunard liner became perhaps the second most infamous shipwreck in history when she was torpedoed by a German submarine during World War I, three years after the *Titanic* disaster. *Lusitania,* you will recall, was one of the White Star Line's great competitors. She was on her way from New York to Liverpool on May 7, 1915, when the torpedo sent her down in 300 feet of water. Almost 2,000 people were on board: 1,200 perished. Because she carried hundreds of Americans—including millionaire Alfred Vanderbilt—her sinking probably did more than anything else to spur America to enter the war against the Germans. (America officially allied with Britain and France two years later to help defeat Germany.)

- *Eastland.* Less than three months after the sinking of *Lusitania,* an excursion steamer with more than 2,000 people aboard "turned turtle," killing 835. Her ballast (the weight inside the hull) wasn't distributed properly, causing the ship to capsize without warning. The astounding thing about *Eastland* is that she wasn't going anywhere when this happened. In fact, she was nowhere near the open ocean: she was tied up at a dock in Chicago, Illinois. In terms of lives lost, the capsizing of *East-land* was the worst disaster in Great Lakes history.

- ***Britannic.*** This third "sister" to *Titanic* and *Olympic* was the largest of the three White Star Line ships. World War I broke out as she was being completed in early 1915, so the British government turned *Britannic* into a hospital ship. Less than two years later, either a mine or a torpedo caused an explosion that sent *Britannic* to the bottom of the Aegean Sea. Remarkably, only 30 of the 1,100 people aboard were lost. But *Britannic* still bears the notorious distinction of being the world's largest ship-wreck. It's worth noting that some of the safety advances suggested after the *Titanic* investigations—a double hull and higher bulkheads, for instance—were incorporated into *Britannic*. Nevertheless, this new, improved liner sank in even less time than it took *Titanic* to go down!

- ***Morro Castle.*** Fire is a constant concern aboard ships. Even though fire may not destroy a vessel's metal sides and cause her to sink, it threatens those trapped aboard with a terrible death. *Morro Castle* was steaming along the eastern seacoast toward New York after a trip to Cuba when she caught fire mysteriously (some blamed sabotage by a crew member) in the predawn hours of September 8, 1934. Weathering a storm, she was within sight of the lights along the New Jersey coast, about 20 miles from the entrance to New York Harbor. More than 130 people died before the smoldering ship was beached near Asbury Park, New Jersey.

- ***Andrea Doria.*** Perhaps a seafarer's worst fear is collision with another vessel. One of the most famous of these catastrophes during the 20th century was the wreck of *Andrea Doria* and *Stockholm*. *Andrea Doria*, an Italian ocean liner, was coming into New York from Europe in a heavy fog on July 25, 1956, when it was struck by the Swedish *Stockholm* off of Nantucket, Massachusetts. *Stockholm*'s bow had been reinforced to

Smoke pours from the liner Morro Castle *as it is beached near Asbury Park, New Jersey. More than 130 people lost their lives in this tragic shipboard fire.*

cope with icy seas: it bored a huge hole into the side of *Andrea Doria*, which sank 11 hours later. Interestingly, both ships were equipped with radar. However, *Andrea Doria*'s navigator could not tell from the radar which direction *Stockholm* was traveling. He thought she was moving away, but she was actually approaching his ship on a collision course!

(Despite the fog and the darkness, *Andrea Doria* was moving at approximately 22 knots—the same speed as *Titanic*.)

- **Thresher.** Many people who aren't afraid to travel on a surface ship would be deathly afraid to do so on a submarine. While submarines have excellent overall safety records, they also pose unique hazards. The U.S. atomic submarine *Thresher* was mysteriously lost during test dives in deep water off New England on April 10, 1963. The most troubling aspect of the *Thresher* disaster, which claimed 129 lives, is that we probably will never know exactly why it happened. A plausible theory is that a pipe fitting burst as the sub neared its test depth. The deeper the water, the greater its "weight" on a vessel. Water, under tremendous pressure at a great depth, probably entered one compartment and made it impossible to bring the craft back to the surface.

- **Exxon Valdez.** Some maritime catastrophes aren't costly in terms of human life, but cause inestimable environmental damage. On March 24, 1989, the supertanker *Exxon Valdez* grounded on Bligh Reef in Prince William Sound, Alaska. She was transporting oil from Alaska down the Pacific coast to California. The 987-foot tanker (more than 100 feet longer than *Titanic*) spilled 11 million gallons of crude oil into the sea. It was the worst oil spill in U.S. history to date. Cleanup of the sound cost billions of dollars; the resulting legal battles lasted for years. One positive result of the *Exxon Valdez* tragedy was the purchase of two "tractor tugs" by oil companies to escort tankers through the sound.

Despite occasional catastrophes, most people today don't fear shipwrecks as travelers of the early 1900s did. Other kinds of disasters—most notably airline accidents—are both more commonplace and more sensational today.

(continued from p. 103)

*   *   *

There will probably never be another disaster like that of *Titanic*, with its massive loss of life resulting from an iceberg collision. Still, no form of travel will ever be completely risk free. Larger vehicles tend to carry graver risks. *Titanic* historian Logan Marshall wrote the following about the huge ocean liners of his day: "The danger lies in their own power—in the tens of thousands of horse power with which they may be driven into another ship or into an iceberg standing cold and unyielding as a wall of granite." Marshall stated the tragic reality demonstrated by the *Titanic* disaster. "If boats are unsinkable as well as fireproof there is no need of any life-boats at all. But no such steamship has ever been constructed," he wrote.

Apart from improvements in shipbuilding and safety, another reason nautical disasters of the *Titanic*'s magnitude no longer occur is that the age of the gigantic liner that could hold legions of passengers has ended. After more than a century of competition to build the fastest and most elegant vessel, Atlantic crossings by ship became impractical. Twenty-two years after the disaster, the Cunard and White Star companies were forced to merge, jointly operating famous passenger ships like *Queen Mary*. The development of international air travel made the days of passenger ships obsolete. Jet planes can now make the trip between England and the United States in about seven hours, offering passengers lower fares than ships, because sea voyages entail paying for days of rooms and meals.

The great American liner *United States*, a "floating palace" like *Titanic*, was launched in 1952 and basked

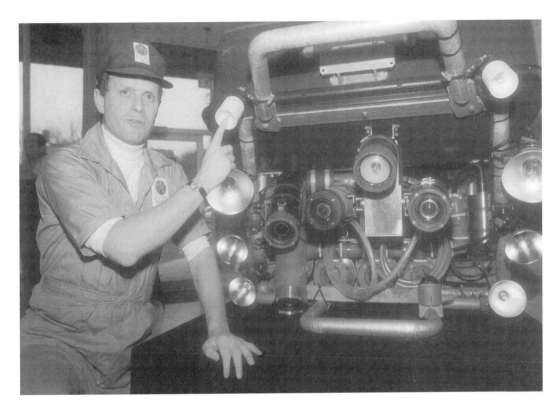

briefly in the bright light of fame. Traveling as fast as 36 knots, it captured the legendary Blue Riband for record passage time on its maiden voyage. *United States* crossed the ocean in less than three-and-a-half days—10 hours faster than the previous record set by England's famous *Queen Mary* during the 1930s.

Ten years later airline service had proven itself safe and reliable. *United States* consequently lost money on most of its later voyages. In 1969 the ship was put in mothballs. The great transatlantic liners had served their purpose and were rapidly vanishing from the seas.

Walter Lord, author of two excellent books about the *Titanic* sinking (*A Night to Remember* and *The Night Lives On*), observes that "there have been massive changes in the world since 1912. We don't even cross

Dr. Robert Ballard points out features of an underwater robot that is similar to the one he used to find and photograph *Titanic*'s remains in 1985.

Southampton, England, has several memorials to those who lost their lives on *Titanic,* including this one dedicated to the ship's engineers, which drew a large crowd at its unveiling in April 1914.

the ocean the same way now, and two great wars have numbed us to casualty lists. Compared to the implications of a nuclear confrontation, the figures of 'souls lost' in a shipwreck—any shipwreck—seem almost quaint."

For many years after its sinking, *Titanic* was sought by undersea researchers. Their painstaking probes were futile until the early morning hours of September 1, 1985. That was when the underwater cameras of a geological team led by Dr. Robert Ballard began photographing pieces of debris, both large and small, over a broad area of ocean floor. It was soon clear that the items, two-and-a-half miles down, could only be from the great liner.

Ballard himself descended to investigate the wreck

the following summer in a research minisubmarine, *Alvin*.

For three-quarters of a century, the *Titanic* tragedy was the subject of widespread debate. Today a new firestorm of controversy swirls around the ship's remains. A year after Ballard and his crew explored the wreck site in *Alvin,* adventurous researchers from the United States and other countries began removing thousands of artifacts from *Titanic*.

The recovered objects were intriguing: fine china, jewelry, a passenger's wallet with his calling card preserved after almost a century in the frigid North Atlantic depths. But the artifact collectors were criticized by oceanographers like Ballard—and by *Titanic* survivors. "The grave should be left alone," said Eva Hart of London, who was seven when she escaped the great liner in a lifeboat.

Titanic is today, in a sense, an undersea museum. It is a reminder that no human design or construction is perfect. With each passing generation, it continues to teach us.

The silent story it tells is timeless. As Walter Lord wrote, "The *Titanic* is always news."

A Chronology of *Titanic*'s History

1899:   Morgan Robertson's novel about a great sea disaster, *The Wreck of the Titan, or Futility,* is published

1900–14: More than 13 million immigrants enter the United States. Most come from Europe to New York

1909:   Construction of *Titanic* begins in the Harland and Wolff Shipyard, Belfast, Ireland

1910:   *Olympic,* the sister ship to *Titanic,* is launched from the Harland and Wolff Shipyard in Belfast

1911:   The hull of *Titanic* is launched on May 31

1912:   Construction is finished on the interior of *Titanic*; E. J. Smith is selected as *Titanic*'s captain; *Titanic* successfully passes its sea trial on April 2; more than 1,500 die after *Titanic* hits an iceberg at 11:40 P.M. on April 14 and sinks beneath the North Atlantic at 2:20 A.M. April 15

1955:   *A Night to Remember,* by Walter Lord, is published

1985:   Robert Ballard leads a team of oceanographers that find the sunken wreck of *Titanic* more than two miles beneath the ocean's surface

1987:   A French oceanographic expedition makes 32 dives on *Titanic* in August, recovering 1,800 objects and taking over 7,000 photographs of the wreck site

1996:   An international scientific research team examines *Titanic* for a month to attempt to solve mysteries surrounding the disaster. The researchers disprove the long-held theory that the iceberg caused a long slash along *Titanic*'s hull, discovering instead that the openings were a series of six thin slits, totaling no more than 12 square feet. The researchers also determine why and how *Titanic* broke in half during the sinking.

1998:   The Titanic Research and Recovery Expedition brings a 20-ton section of the ship's outer hull to the surface.

1999:   The large piece of *Titanic*'s hull, along with thousands of other artifacts, are exhibited in the United States and throughout the world.

A Chronology of *Titanic*'s Maiden Voyage in April 1912

April 10:

> 12 P.M.: *Titanic*'s maiden voyage begins; ship nearly nearly hit by drifting liner *New York* as it exits harbor

> 7 P.M.: *Titanic* arrives in Cherbourg, France, to pick up passengers, leaves two hours later for Queenstown, Ireland.

April 11:

> 2 P.M.: *Titanic* leaves Queenstown, Ireland, headed for America.

April 12–13: *Titanic*'s captain receives ice warnings.

April 14:

> 11 P.M.: Final iceberg warning received from *Californian*

> 11:35 P.M.: the wireless set aboard *Californian* is turned off, preventing further communication with *Titanic*

> 11:40 P.M.: *Titanic* collides with an iceberg

April 15:

> 12:35 A.M.: *Carpathia* receives distress signals from *Titanic* and changes its course to try and provide assistance

> 1:50 A.M.: Final distress signal is received by *Carpathia*

> 2:05 A.M.: *Titanic*'s last lifeboat is lowered into the sea

> 2:20 A.M.: The stern rail of *Titanic* sinks completely beneath the surface

> 4:00 A.M.: *Carpathia* arrives at the disaster scene to rescue *Titanic* survivors

> 8 A.M.: *Californian* arrives as *Carpathia* is preparing to depart for New York.

April 16: *Titanic* survivors arrive in New York.

Further Reading

Brown, E. W. *The Modern Industries Series: Ships.* Exeter, Great Britain: A. Wheaton and Company, 1965.

Butler, Daniel Allen. *"Unsinkable": The Full Story of RMS Titanic.* Mechanicsburg, Pa.: Stackpole Books, 1998.

Chaffee, Allen. *Heroes of the Shoals.* New York: Henry Holt and Company, 1935.

Davie, Michael. *Titanic: The Death and Life of a Legend.* New York: Alfred A. Knopf, 1987.

Garrison, Webb. *A Treasury of Titanic Tales.* Nashville, Tenn.: Rutledge Hill Press, 1998.

Gracie, Colonel Archibald. *Titanic: A Survivor's Story.* Chicago: Academy Chicago Publishers, 1998. (Reprint of 1913 book originally entitled *The Truth About the Titanic.*)

Hoehling, A. A. *They Sailed into Oblivion.* New York: Ace Books, 1959.

Hudson, Kenneth, and Ann Nicholls. *Tragedy on the High Seas.* New York: A&W Publishers, Inc., 1979.

Lobley, Douglas. *Ships Through the Ages.* Secaucus, N.J.: Derbibooks, 1975.

Lord, Walter. *A Night to Remember.* New York: Holt, Rinehart & Winston, Inc., 1955.

———. *The Night Lives On.* New York: William Morrow and Company, Inc., 1986.

Lynch, Don, and Ken Marschall. *Titanic: An Illustrated History.* New York: Hyperion, 1992.

Maddocks, Melvin, et al. *The Seafarers: The Atlantic Crossing.* Alexandria, Va.: Time-Life Books, 1981.

Further Reading

————. *The Seafarers: The Great Liners.* Alexandria, Va.: Time-Life Books, 1978.

Marcus, Geoffrey. *The Maiden Voyage.* New York: Manor Books, 1977.

Marshall, Logan. *The Sinking of the Titanic.* Seattle: Hara Publishing, 1996. (Abridged edition of original 1912 publication.)

Maxtone-Graham, John. *The Only Way to Cross.* New York: Collier Books, 1972.

McKinlay, William Laird. *Karluk: The Great Untold Story of Arctic Exploration.* New York: St. Martin's Press, 1976.

O'Donnell, E. E. *The Last Days of the Titanic: Photographs and Mementos of the Tragic Maiden Voyage.* Niwot, Colo.: Roberts Rinehart Publishers, 1997.

Phillips-Birt, Douglas. *A History of Seamanship.* Garden City, N.Y.: Doubleday & Company, 1971.

Robertson, Morgan. *The Wreck of the Titan, or Futility.* Riverside, Conn.: 7 C's Press, 1974. (Reprint.)

Snow, Edward Rowe. *Sea Disasters and Inland Catastrophes.* New York: Dodd, Mead & Company, 1980.

————. *Unsolved Mysteries of Sea and Shore.* New York: Dodd, Mead & Company, 1963.

Wade, Wyn Craig. *The Titanic: End of a Dream.* New York: Rawson, Wade Publishers, 1979.

Wels, Susan. *Titanic: Legacy of the World's Greatest Ocean Liner.* Del Mar, Calif.: Tehabi Books, 1997.

Index

Adriatic, 25
Air travel, 107, 108, 109
Allen Line, 67
Alvin, 111
American Red Cross, 77
American Tobacco Company, 34
Andrea Doria, 106–7
Andrews, Thomas, 42–43, 50–51, 56, 86
Asbury Park, New Jersey, 106
Astor, John Jacob, 17, 38, 40, 55, 79
Astor, Madeline, 17, 38, 40

Ballard, Robert, 63, 110
Baltic, 41
Belfast, Ireland, 13, 14
Bigham, John Charles, 88
Birma, 68
Blue Riband, the, 109
Bride, Harold, 50, 59, 75, 84
Britannic, 20–21, 105–6
British Board of Trade, 71, 83, 84, 85, 88–92
British Royal Navy, 11
Brown, Margaret, 54–55
Bulkheads. *See* Watertight compartments
Burgess, Charles, 34–35
Butt, Archibald, 40, 55

Californian, 68–70, 71, 73, 84, 85, 86–87, 92–93, 99–100, 101

Canada, 45, 67
Cape Race, Newfoundland, 51, 69
Carpathia, 23, 68, 71–79, 83, 84, 85, 87, 94, 103
Cherbourg, France, 38
Chicago, Illinois, 105
Columbus, Christopher, 13
Cottam, Harold, 71
Cuba, 106
Cunard Line, 20, 23, 28, 35, 68, 77, 94, 104, 108

Denver, Colorado, 54
Distress signals, 51, 59, 67, 87, 99–101
Duff-Gordon, Cosmo, 38, 89
Duff-Gordon, Lucille, 38

Eastland, 104–5
Edward VII (king of England), 102
Edwardian era, 102
Elizabeth Lines, 95
Ellis Island, 77
England, 20, 35, 54, 68, 74, 82, 83, 88, 92, 102, 104, 108, 109
"Englehardts," 27
Evans, Cyril, 69–70
Exxon Valdez, 107

Fleet, Frederick, 45, 47–48, 49, 93
France, 20, 104
Frankfurt, 68

Futrelle, Jacques, 40, 56

Germany, 20, 104
Gigantic. See *Britannic*
Gilded Age, the, 23
Greenland, 41
Guggenheim, Benjamin, 17, 34, 56

Harland and Wolff company, 42
Harper, Henry Sleeper, 40
Harper & Brothers, 40
Hawke, 26
Hays, Charles M., 40, 56

Icebergs, 12, 25, 26, 29, 30–31, 41–42, 45, 47–50, 51, 82, 85, 93, 94, 97, 99
International Ice Patrol, 99
International Mercantile Marine, 97
Isle of Wight, England, 26
Ismay, J. Bruce, 39–40, 43, 71, 75–76, 83–84, 86, 89, 95, 98
Italy, 20

Joughin, Charles, 55–56

Karluk, 31

La Provence, 68
Lee, Reginald, 48, 49
Leyland Line, 69, 93
Lichfield, England, 95

Lifeboats, 12, 26–30, 52–56, 57, 58, 59–60, 62, 63, 64–65, 66, 71, 72–73, 76, 79, 83, 84–85, 86, 87, 88, 89, 90–92, 97, 98–99, 102, 103, 108
Lightoller, Charles, 52, 57, 63–64, 84, 85, 88–89, 93
Liverpool, England, 104
London, England, 88, 111
Loran, 101
Lord, Stanley, 70, 84, 85, 92–93
Lord, Walter, 92–93, 109–10, 111
Lusitania, 20, 104
Lynch, Don, 48–49

McKinlay, William Laird, 31
Macy's department store, 34
Maddocks, Melvin, 104
Marconi's Wireless Telegraph Company, 100, 101
Marshall, Logan, 52, 90–91, 98–99, 108
Mauretania, 20
Mayflower, 13
Mersey, Lord, 88, 89, 92
Mesaba, 45
Millet, Francis David, 40, 56
Morro Castle, 106
Morse code, 41
Mt. Temple, 68

Murdoch, William, 47–50, 59, 60

Nantucket, Massachusetts, 106
Newfoundland, 45, 51, 65, 71, 98
New Jersey, 106
Newlands, Francis, 83
New York, 35–37, 60
New York City, 23, 34, 39, 68, 75, 76–77, 78, 86, 94, 95, 104, 106
Night Lives On, The (Lord), 109–10
Night to Remember, A (Lord), 109–10
Nina, 13
Norway, 71

Olympic, 20–21, 26, 35, 68, 75, 95, 105
Orchestra, 35, 56–57

Pennsylvania Railroad, 40, 77
Peuchen, Arthur, 63
Phillips, J. G., 45, 50, 59, 68, 69
Pilgrims, 13
Pitman, Herbert, 94
Prince William Sound, Alaska, 107

Queen Mary, 108, 109
Queenstown, Ireland, 38

Radar, 101, 106

Radios, 40–41, 45, 50, 59, 67, 68, 69–70, 74, 77, 78, 86, 87, 99–101
River Test, 35
Robertson, Morgan, 13, 14, 17
Rostron, Arthur H., 68, 71–72, 75–76, 77–78, 79, 94
Ryerson, Emily, 95

Salvation Army, 77
Samson, 71
Senate, U.S., 83, 84, 85, 87, 92, 97, 99, 100, 111
Sims, William S., 98
Smith, Edward J., 21, 23, 25, 26, 28–29, 38, 39, 41, 43, 50–52, 60–62, 70, 71, 83, 84, 85, 86, 88, 89, 94, 95
Smith, William Alden, 83–87, 88, 99, 100–1, 102
SOS distress signal, 51, 101
Southampton, England, 13, 16, 33, 48, 91
Steerage passengers, 20, 23, 34, 57, 74, 77, 86, 89, 90, 103
Stockholm, S.S., 106
Straus, Harry, 17, 34, 40
Straus, Ida, 17, 34, 40
Straus, Isidor, 17, 34, 40, 56
Submarines, 107
Sweden, 20

Index

Thayer, Jack, 40, 45
Thayer, John B., 40, 56
Titanic,
   construction of, 13–21,
     24–26, 105
   exploration for wreck-
     age, 63, 87, 110–11
   inquiries into sinking,
     81–95, 99
   maiden voyage, 21,
     28–29, 33–63
   rescue of passengers,
     67–79
   sinking of, 12–13, 29,
     47–63
Titanic: An Illustrated His-
   tory (Lynch), 48–49

Titanic Historical Society,
   48

Underwater explorations,
   63, 87, 110–11
United States, 108–9
United States Steel Cor-
   poration, 34
"Unsinkable Molly
   Brown, the." *See* Mar-
   garet Brown

Vanderbilt, Alfred G., 104
Virginian, 67

Waldorf-Astoria Hotel,
   84

Watertight compart-
   ments, 12, 14, 15,
   24–25, 26, 50–51, 87, 91
White Star Steamship
   Line, 13, 16, 17, 20, 24,
   25, 26, 28, 29, 30, 38,
   39, 41, 42, 43, 75, 79,
   86, 91, 93, 98, 100, 103,
   104, 108
Widener, George, D., 17,
   34, 40, 43
"Wireless." *See* Radio
World War I, 104, 105–6

Ypiranga, 68

Picture Credits

page

2-3: Archive Photos
10: Archive Photos
14: Archive Photos
15: Brown Brothers
18: AP/Wide World Photos
22: Brown Brothers
27: Titanic Historical Society
28: Archive Photos
30: Archive Photos
32-33: AP/Wide World Photos
36-37: Brown Brothers
39: Corbis-Bettmann
40: Titanic Historical Society
43: Titanic Historical Society

44: Corbis-Bettmann
46: Corbis-Bettmann
48: Titanic Historical Society
49: Titanic Historical Society
53: Archive Photos
54: Corbis-Bettmann
58: Archive Photos
61: Archive Photos
66: Archive Photos
69: Corbis-Bettmann
75: Brown Brothers
76: Brown Brothers
78: Archive Photos
80-81: Corbis-Bettmann

82: Corbis-Bettmann
85: Titanic Historical Society
90: Brown Brothers
93: Titanic Historical Society
94: Illustration by Takeshi Takahashi
96: Archive Photos
100: Archive Photos
103: Corbis
106: AP/Wide World Photos
109: AP/Wide World Photos
110: Archive Photos

DAN HARMON is an editor and writer living in Spartanburg, South Carolina. He has written several books on humor and history, and has contributed historical and cultural articles to the *New York Times, Music Journal, Nautilus,* and many other periodicals. He is the managing editor of *Sandlapper: The Magazine of South Carolina* and is editor of *The Lawyer's PC* newsletter. His books include *Civil War Leaders* and *Fighting Units of the American War of Independence.*

JILL McCAFFREY has served for four years as national chairman of the Armed Forces Emergency Services of the American Red Cross. Ms. McCaffrey also serves on the board of directors for Knollwood—the Army Distaff Hall. The former Jill Ann Faulkner, a Massachusetts native, is the wife of Barry R. McCaffrey, a member of President Bill Clinton's cabinet and director of the White House Office of National Drug Control Policy. The McCaffreys are the parents of three grown children: Sean, a major in the U.S. Army; Tara, an intensive care nurse and captain in the National Guard; and Amy, a seventh grade teacher. The McCaffreys also have two grandchildren, Michael and Jack.